Wrestling
with
Crocodiles

Stuart Wineberg

Wrestling
with
Crocodiles

Matador
9 De Montfort Mews
Leicester LE1 7FW, UK
Tel: (+44) 116 255 9311 / 9312
Email: books@troubador.co.uk
Web: www.troubador.co.uk/matador

ISBN 978 1906221 669

Typeset in 11pt Gill Sans by Troubador Publishing Ltd, Leicester, UK
Printed and bound in Great Britain by Cromwell Press, Trowbridge, Wiltshire

Matador is an imprint of Troubador Publishing Ltd

For my father, Mitchell.
He would have been both surprised and delighted to see this book.

What people say about Stuart's workshops and presentations ...

"Stuart was fantastic! What a guy! Not only does he manage to get the information across in such a way that really sticks, he is also a wonderful entertainer."

"I feel much more confident that I was presenting what I wanted the group to know. Thank you"

"By far the best presentation skills session I have been on (and I have been on a few). Very much in the real world."

"Fantastic, relevant, lots of practical tips. Very entertaining"

"Useful, well presented, attractive. 5 stars"

"Stuart continues to provide a creative format and still get all relevant points across. He's fab".

"So much fantastic feedback and extensive real life knowledge."

"10/10. Great teaching skills, huge knowledge. The course has been a real pleasure"

"Everyone who is intending to deliver a presentation should do this course"

"An excellent course for people at all levels of experience. Go for it."

This is a small sample of the positive and generous comments given to me following my workshops. If you would like to see the originals anytime or send me feedback on *Wrestling with Crocodiles* please get in touch, I would love to hear from you.

Email me at stuart@bluestone-training.com

Contents

Acknowledgements

I knew writing a book wouldn't be easy. I also knew I wanted to write this book.

I am luckier than most authors. I have a successful business as a trainer and consultant and my challenge wasn't to find a way to pay the bills whilst I wrote this, it was to find time and space in a demanding schedule.

That's why my first and most important acknowledgment is to my wife Jenny and my daughter Ali who have done everything they can to take the pressure off me whilst I was huddled away in the office. My Mother also deserves thanks for entertaining and feeding us and joining in the chorus of voices trying to stop me overworking.

Several people have read and commented on early drafts of the book and as well as their time, I appreciate the encouragement that they have all given me to carry on to the finish. Foremost amongst these is my friend Liz Clark. Liz sets my standard for self-belief and the need to strive to be the best in whatever endeavour I undertake. Her friendly but ferocious comments on the book should really earn her a credit as editor. Other significant comments have come from James Hodgson and my brother-in-law Malcolm Colling.

Malcolm, an accomplished author in his own right, also deserves thanks for introducing me to the morass that is the world of book publishers, agents and distributors.

Finally, the wonderful Ricky Thaxter. I have worked with Ricky for several years now and his ability to take my vague verbal briefs or rough sketches and turn them into dazzling artwork is remarkable. I described the crocodile to Ricky over the phone one morning a year

or so ago and the reptile emerged fully formed from an email attach-
ment about two hours later. If you would like to work with Ricky, you
can contact him on DeepasU@aol.com

Where mentioned, trade names are the copyright of the owners.

No crocodiles were harmed during the production of this book.

As I (inevitably) get older, I realise how lucky I am. Successful people
make the most of their luck but there is no doubt that I have learnt
to appreciate some simple things in life that other people can only
dream about. Some of these are that I have always had a warm, dry
place to live and as much food as I can eat.

I invest a lot of my spare time in supporting the Rotary Foundation –
one of the world's largest charitable organisations. As a result, I have
had the privilege of bringing a small amount of help to some of the
most deprived people in the world, so I thought that I would use this
book to address a need closer to home.

A proportion of the proceeds from this book will go to the Society
of St. James, which works to provide shelter and support to homeless
people in the part of Hampshire where I live.

Introduction

Wrestling with crocodiles

One of the delegates at the start of my workshop "Presenting With Confidence" told us that he would rather wrestle with a crocodile than present in public. 2 days later after he finished his final presentation, in polished, confident and impactful style, he was asked for his feelings about the workshop – "I am delighted to say I would now rather present than wrestle with a croc". Ever since then, my stated objective for the workshops is to have my delegates happier to present than to fight an agitated potential handbag.

All through this book you will find that the crocodile has become your friend, pointing the way to good ideas and brightening up the text. He has become so popular that he is now without a doubt my personal and professional mascot.

Why Did I Write This Book?

Over the past 15 years, I have had the privilege of helping hundreds of people all over the world to develop their professional presentation skills through my two-day workshop "Presenting With Confidence". I have gained huge satisfaction from watching the change in skill level and confidence that occurs over those two days. Unfortunately, I can only reach a limited number of people through these workshops and it was suggested to me that the techniques I use would lend themselves to a short, practical book of advice that could help a wider audience.

Who is this book for?

Some of the people reading this book may be experienced professional presenters who routinely tackle challenging business presentations as part of their day-to-day job. You may be seeking some hints, tips and suggestions to add to your experience. Some of you may rarely or never present and have the prospect of facing an audience for the first time in recent years. You may be searching for any support and practical advice that I can give you.

Whatever your experience, this book will build on it and help you achieve the best possible outcome for the presentation you are about to give.

If you do not have a presentation to prepare and present in the near future – say within the next three months; then wait until you do. This book is at its best supporting you through the real experience. Presenting skills aren't a theoretical piece of knowledge, they are practical skills and you need to take the advice given here and use it if you want to become an effective presenter.

This book is for:

*   Experienced presenters who want to polish their style and learn some more useful practical tips

*   Inexperienced presenters searching for a wealth of practical ideas to use as they face an audience

*   People who have a presentation to prepare and deliver within the next three months

How to use this book

I hope that when you invite me to lunch and you produce your copy of this book, it will be a well-thumbed and battered old friend. Like a well-used recipe book that is splashed with gravy and covered in your thoughts about your favourite food, this book will work best for you when it is personalised.

Read it with a pen and highlighter close by, feel free to turn down corners and write in the margins. I can assure you that the sections of the book that you make your own will stay with you and make the biggest difference to your presentations.

Above all, use it as the basis for action. Standing in front of an audience is primarily a practical exercise. The thoughts and ideas in this book will underpin the way that you develop your skills and will guide you towards the best methods. Ultimately, you will improve most by standing up and speaking and then reflecting on what you learnt from the experience.

After each presentation, ask yourself the questions in the box below and take your time answering, especially with the first question. Write everything down, especially your personal action plan for next time. Take that plan with you to your next presentation.

•   *What went well during your presentation?*

•   *What could have gone even better?*

•   *What have you learned from the experience?*

•   *What specifically, will you do differently next time as a result of this experience?*

Presenting effectively is a wonderful feeling and I have written this book to be fun to work with as well as being both practical and easy to read. Enjoy it.

Meet The Crocs

My friendly crocodile inhabits the pages of this book and has managed to get himself into some rather strange situations. In amongst the humour are some signposts for you.

Presenter croc heads up each chapter. He also appears anywhere there are lists of topics. He will help you navigate around the content of the book.

This book is full of ideas for you to think about. Look out for this top tip croc.

If you follow the advice in this book, there isn't much that can go wrong. However, where there are specific things to be careful about, look out for this cautionary "tail".

When you see this croc, there are some specific actions for you to take. These are often physical techniques. Do take the time to carry these out, as they are the links between the theory and the real world of presenting.

At the end of each chapter, there is a summary of the key points from the preceding pages. These are the things you should be adding to your toolbox.

What Do I Do After I Have Read This Book?

Stuart and his team will be delighted to work with you and your organisation on either an individual or group basis.

We work anywhere in the world and with a wide range of different companies and organisations. To find out how we can help you develop your skills and those of your people, get in touch either by email at:

stuart@bluestone-training.com

or by visiting our website at: **www.bluestone-training.com**

If you would like more copies of this book, please ask for it at your local bookshop or visit our website. We will be delighted to produce customised covers with your company logo or specific messages.

Can I really do this?

Presentations – What a Stupid Way to Communicate

An industry has built up around presentations. Computer software companies have grown rich writing graphics packages. Data projectors, laser pointers and other assorted hardware abound. All of these support a fundamentally flawed way of communicating.

Think about it. Let's imagine you have 20 minutes to present on a technical or business topic to a reasonably well-informed audience. In you walk – you talk for 18 minutes using about 20 images and the audience has to listen to you, take in the images for the first time, decide if they form a logical flow and if they like/dislike/agree/disagree with your conclusion. Then, unless you provide copies, the images are gone forever and you then conduct a rushed question and answer session where the ill-informed audience torments the petrified presenter.

Let's rewind that scene. In you walk with a document for each member of the audience. You hand out the papers.

> *"Ladies and Gentlemen, here are copies of the slides I was planning to show you. Attached to each is a script giving the exact words I was going to use. Here also is a highlighter pen for you to keep. I have a 20 minute time slot. For the next 15 minutes please read the slides and the notes. Compare one slide with another and make sure you are happy with the flow of my ideas. Please talk amongst yourselves and mark up any queries you may have. I am going to get a coffee and I will be back in 15 minutes to chair a short discussion on this material."*

The second approach is more professional, relaxed and a more effective way of communicating. It is also nonsense. We all know that this would never happen even though it would work very well. Why is that? The reason is both simple and also represents one of the fundamental principles of the psychology of effective presenting.

The members of the audience need to judge the speaker before they can judge the content. That's so important that it is going to be one of my tips.

I will return to this subject later but it is an absolute truth and if you find it hard to accept then please trust me for a while and see where my argument takes you.

The audience needs to judge the speaker before they can judge the content

Can I Ever Be A Talented Presenter?

To be honest, I don't know. Talented people are born not made. They usually only express their talent after a lot of hard work. It doesn't matter; this book is not just for talented people. It is for people who want to be effective presenters and you can definitely be one of those.

Think about your audience for a moment. They sit there and take in all sorts of information. They see you and your visual aids. They hear your voice. They handle any materials or items that you give them. That's it – that is everything that constitutes your presentation. From these few pieces of input they come to a very wide range of conclusions. They decide:

- If you are engaging them with steady eye contact

- If you are standing still or walking round

- If you have memorised your material or if you are reading your notes

None of these are surprises. These are concrete things that are evident to any observer. More surprising is that they also decide:

- If you are confident or not

- If you want to be there

- If you are a relaxed presenter

Now this is very interesting. None of the things in this second list are concrete and they are not overtly obvious. Nonetheless every member of the audience will have formed an opinion about them within a few seconds of you standing up.

So here we have one of the most important things for you to understand about presenting. The audience come to all their conclusions about you from the simple things that you say and do. When you understand how this happens you will be able to control what the audience thinks about you by controlling what you physically do in front of them, regardless of how you actually feel inside.

If you behave confidently, the audience will respond positively – regardless of how you feel inside

You are probably thinking that this is all very well but what does confident behaviour look like? Relax – most of the rest of this book is devoted to just this topic. Before we get into that though, there are a couple more points to make.

•   Audiences respond positively to positive behaviour

•   Audiences want to see you do well

If you go out in front of an audience with positive and confident behaviour, they will respond positively. You will see them smile, hear the positive buzz of anticipation and feel the warmth that comes from a group of people who are welcoming you. All of this makes it easy to carry on and a wonderful positive ascending spiral develops and you ride it for the rest of your talk.

However the challenge is that you have to go there first – you have to exhibit the positive behaviours to which they can respond. This means that one of the secrets of effective presenting is to be your best at the start of the presentation. If you need time to warm up, do it in an empty room before the audience arrives.

Audiences want you to do well. It isn't much fun watching someone struggle. Listening to an effective speaker is a pleasure. It allows the audience the opportunity to relax and take in the message. Many speakers worry that they will be challenged by someone in the audience. Here's another vital take away message for you.

Audiences challenge content. They rarely challenge the personality of the presenter

Strong challenges from the audiences are almost always aimed at your material NOT at you. In fact a strong challenge to your material means you have presented well. You have communicated an idea and the audience is sufficiently interested in it to ask searching questions. This is all good news – assuming you know your material.

This book will give you all the tools you need to be the most confident and competent presenter that you want to be. It is designed to be practical and everything in here has been proven to work time and time again with many hundreds of delegates. It will work for you if you believe in the advice and put it into action with real commitment.

Crocodile Summary

- The audience judges the presentation by what it thinks about you

- Anyone can be an effective presenter if they use the right techniques

- Audiences usually challenge content, not your personality

2
I can do it!
What do I do?

Workout time

Here's something to think about. If you stand up in front of an audience and speak for 20 minutes, using supporting visuals but not giving any handouts, the audience will walk away having taken on board no more than three points or ideas.

The audience will only take away three or so ideas from a 20-30 minute presentation

In the absence of any control from you, the three ideas might be that you were wandering around in a distracting way, you were wearing a scarf that they didn't really like and if you are lucky, they might remember something about the content of your presentation.

The point is, that however effective you are as a presenter; you need to be totally aware that you can only communicate three ideas. You also need to be just as aware that it is your responsibility to control what it is that the audience remembers.

The most significant way in which you can achieve this is by making use of the physical presentation techniques that are available to you. In other words, the use of some simple actions such as the well-timed gesture, a pace forward or a change in voice can lock an idea into the mind of your audience.

In order to do this effectively, you need to be completely clear about what it is you are trying to achieve and this will be a subject in its own right later on in the book.

For the moment, concentrate on your physical technique and particularly your use of :

*   Stance

*   Gestures

*   Eye Contact

*   Voice

I'm Just Standing

This has two separate components:

*   How to stand when you are standing still.

*   How and when to move when you want to do so.

Most of the time you should stand still when you are presenting. It works like this. Everything that you say whilst you are moving is lost. The audience will retain their impression of you but will remember very little of what you actually said. This is because visual signals are generally more memorable than auditory ones. So given the choice between listening to your words and watching you move, most people will eventually watch you move. Is this a bad thing? It depends.

If your objective is to motivate a group, to leave them with a positive impression and sense of your dynamism, then moving around can enhance this – especially if you actually move into the audience. You see this a lot in the theatre and on TV and this technique has been greatly aided by the development of tools such as radio microphones. The end result is likely to be a warm positive feeling but the audience probably will not be able to tell you why they feel so positive.

If your objective is to inform, educate or to achieve anything which requires the audience to recall the substance of what you have said, then it is vital to keep still whilst you deliver your key messages. One of the ways that you as the presenter can help decide what the audience recalls is by keeping still whilst you deliver those key messages.

A constantly moving speaker can energise but cannot inform

You need to give yourself a stable base to work from so stand squarely on to your audience. Have your feet about the same width apart as your hips at most. Less is OK but your feet must not touch – this is inherently unstable and you will start to wobble. Too wide looks very aggressive and should also be avoided. Have your weight evenly distributed. If you put your weight on one hip you look sloppy and immediately lack authority. If you are facilitating a discussion or training people and want them to participate and debate with you then a relaxed "one sided" stance can be very effective. This does not look good for a more formal presentation.

At this point in my workshops, I am usually given the challenge that it

Whenever you deliver a key point or important piece of information, make sure you are standing still

would be impossible to stand fixedly like this for 20 minutes. I could not agree more. In order to engage with your audience you will need to move. However, when you are moving STOP TALKING. It takes less than two seconds to walk from one side of a small stage to the other and settle there. As you will find out later, one of the most powerful ways to look confident as a presenter is to use silence. A couple of seconds of quiet whilst you move to address another part of the audience is very powerful. After you have moved, settle into the same stable stance that you had before and then deliver your message.

Crocodile summary

*   Feet hip width apart

*   Well grounded, keeping still

*   Weight evenly distributed

*   Keep quiet when you move

Give me a Hand

Quite a few of the people who come to my workshops tell me that they have been instructed by previous trainers not to use gestures as they are distracting. I have to disagree. Used well, gestures are your most powerful tool as a presenter after your voice. However, gestures have to be relevant and purposeful. I completely agree that someone flailing around randomly is not adding to the impact of his or her talk.

The advantage of gestures as a communication tool is that they can be delivered at the same level as the face. In this way they can be congruent with the verbal message that you are delivering. If they are used in this way they add focus and a powerful kind of visual punctuation to your presentation.

Just as with how to stand, there are two aspects to effective use of gestures:

- How to use your hands between gestures

- How to use gestures effectively

How to use your hands between gestures

In the same way that silence is a vital part of using the voice well, pauses in the flow of gestures are also a way of refreshing your impact on the audience. In order to achieve this you need to develop a resting position for your hands. For most people this is in one of two places, either with your hands hanging loosely down by your side or clasped gently together just above your waist. These are equally effective and experienced presenters will use both to ensure that they do not look too repetitive.

It is worth taking a moment to consider each of these resting positions.

The position with the hands hanging loosely by the sides is simple and easy to achieve since it relies solely on gravity. It looks relaxed and it presents an open aspect to the audience, which looks confident. Its disadvantages are that it is a long way to move from this resting position to a positive gesture at the level of the face. As a result, many people lose courage and instead deliver a small twitch of the hand without moving up to a full gesture.

Try this now. Stand facing a full-length mirror. Make sure your feet are slightly apart as you learned in the last section and let your hands fall loosely to your sides. Take a moment to think about how you look. Do not judge the effect by how you feel. This is probably something that you have never done before and the position will feel rather strange. Remember also that in the real situation of a presentation, you would only hold this position for a maximum of 2 seconds and you are watching yourself for much longer than that.

Just before you break this position, try this demonstration of the importance of making a positive movement from this position to a full gesture. Hold the resting position and start to twitch just one finger to as small an extent as you can. You may be surprised to see how distracting and visible this tiny movement can be. This is why you must either let your hand hang free and motionless or make a positive, meaningful gesture to support your message.

Now consider the other alternative. This is based on the way that TV presenters always used to place their hands until the recent fashion for showing the presenter full-length whilst he or she is usually perched on a gantry somewhere with a clipboard and a headset microphone.

The reason for this resting position with the hands clasped loosely just above the waist is that almost every TV camera shot was from top of head to waist and it is important for someone who is framed in that way to keep their hands in the picture. As a result we have become conditioned to interpret this hand position as professional.

As well as appearing professional, it has the advantage of requiring only a short distance to move from the resting position to a full gesture. It does, however, also present some challenges. Firstly it is a closed position, with the centre part of the body covered and this can look defensive, so it is very important not to hold this position for too long. Secondly, if the hands are turned upwards so that the palms are cupped, it can make the presenter look as if they are pleading for mercy much like an escapee from a Charles Dickens orphanage.

The most important challenge though, is to overcome what I call the superglue effect. This is the way in which as soon as the presenter's hands touch, there is a tendency for the loose grasp to become a tight grip that can last through the whole presentation. This prevents any further gestures, builds up tension in the shoulders and inhibits breathing.

Despite the challenges and practice required to make this technique seem natural, this is the most effective hand position for most presenters:

> *Try this now. Stand facing a full-length mirror and again make sure your feet are slightly apart. This time hold your hands together in a loose grasp. The most comfortable way will depend on the natural angles of your arms and wrists. Take a moment to think about how you look.*

Make sure that you avoid:

•   Praying hands

•   Cupped hands

•   Hands drooping down lower than your wrists

Once more do not judge the effect by how you feel – this is probably something you have never done before and the position will feel rather strange.

Now that you have a choice of useful two second resting positions, it is time to think about the gestures themselves. The issues to consider here are:

• Size of gesture

• Shape of gesture

• Hand position

• Asymmetry

Size of gesture

We often overestimate the size of our movements. As a result, many delegates are concerned that they are using excessively large gestures and they may look stupid. I always reply that they should try to use expansive gestures and that if they are too large, I promise to let them know and we can reduce the size. Despite keeping strictly to my promise, I spend far more time working with people to open up their gestures than I do trying to get them to scale down.

So how big should gestures be? Simple – they should be large enough to encompass the people at the outer edges of your audience. So, if you are speaking to six people, a narrow span of gestures is fine. If you are speaking to five hundred or more then you will have to gesture outwards and probably upwards as well to involve everyone.

Gestures begin at the outer edge of your body line and go outwards from there. Many people use a range that is from the centre of their body to the edge and after a few minutes they look like they are having a private conversation that is designed to exclude the audience.

Expressive gestures are driven from your shoulder not from your elbow. Many people use a good range of gestures but do so in a way that I call "pinned" with the elbows firmly against their sides. The effect is closely reminiscent of a penguin.

Gestures should also operate broadly at head height. There are many exceptions to this rule and you should use a wide range of gestures to add to the interest of what you do, but they should mostly be above the waist and roughly at the level of your mouth.

Shape of Gesture

Once we have dealt with the size of gestures, the next thing I am always asked is "What should I actually do with my hands?"

With practice, using your hands in a flowing expressive way will become much more natural. The best way to start off the process of learning to use a range of gestures is to literally paint what you are saying in the air. Think about your message and decide how to illustrate it with your hands. For instance:

- If you want to describe the idea of all of something, you can make the shape of a globe in the air with both hands

- If you want to describe how something moved from one place to another, indicate where it started and as you describe the movement, use the other hand to show the end point

- If one piece of information was bigger than another, indicate their relative heights with your hands as if you were demonstrating the sizes of histogram bars on a graph.

I frequently teach scientists and doctors to present and one of my key messages to these audiences is that words are not a good tool for communicating detailed numerical information. If you really do need your audience to remember the data you are describing then you must give them a handout or make the piece of data the one key message in your talk. Simply to say "44% of patients were cured with treatment A and 56% with treatment B" is not memorable and the numbers will be quickly forgotten.

On the other hand, gestures are powerful tools for demonstrating relativities. So if you were to say "Treatment A cured fewer people than treatment B" and at the same time indicating the relative cure rates by one gesture lower than the other, the hand movements are very memorable and the relative merits of A vs B will be recalled long after the numbers are forgotten.

Hand Position

Hand position is important in gesturing. It is easy to give the wrong impression.

A gesture that brings your hands into an upward facing, cupped position will make you seem to be begging and will be interpreted by your audience as being rather weak.

Pointing is accusatory and aggressive. Whilst most people are aware of this many hold their hands loosely and in a way that allows the index finger to come forward and appear to be pointing.

If the palm of the hand faces the audience then this appears to be rejecting or pushing the audience away and creates an unintended barrier. You can use this to your advantage in dealing with someone who asks repeated questions. To reduce the risk that she will ask yet another question, walk towards the person, smile and as you ask her if she has anything else to ask, gently gesture with your palm facing towards her. The movement should be into her peripheral vision, not directly towards the face. The combination of the smile and the question (all positive) combined with the movement and the gesture (both negative) is confusing and tends to stop further interruptions.

So, what is the best way to make positive gestures? I use a technique that I call the pint of beer gesture, but feel free to call it the gin and tonic or white wine gesture if you prefer.

Imagine that your favourite drink is hovering in the air between you and the person you want to engage with. As you address the person, engage him with steady eye contact and reach out to take the drink and bring it back towards you. Because you don't want to spill this imaginary drink, your gesture will be soft and flowing and the effect will be to draw the person towards you and involve him in what you are saying.

Asymmetry

Much of the impact in a presentation comes from changes and shifts in any of the techniques you are using. Symmetrical gestures, where both hands make the same movements at the same time, often repeatedly, can both bore the audience and lack impact in terms of communicating an idea effectively. Always strive to bring asymmetry into what you do. You can achieve this by:

*   Letting one had drop to your side momentarily whilst you make a point with the other hand

*   Crossing over your centre line – in other words gesturing towards something on the left side of your body but using your right hand

*   Being aware of three-dimensional space. Occasionally gesturing above or below your head height to make a point and even towards the screen to emphasise an idea

Try this energiser either with a friend or again looking at your reflection in the mirror.

> *Think of a wild animal (a crocodile if you like). Now describe it to your mythical five year-old nephew who has only ever seen a dog, cat and guinea-pig. Use your hands to describe the creature rather than compli-cated verbal descriptions. That should open up your gestures for you.*

Put Your Brain in Three Places

A final thought about gestures is the need for you to develop an awareness of where your body is and where the audience and your equipment are. Hence the idea of having your brain in three places.

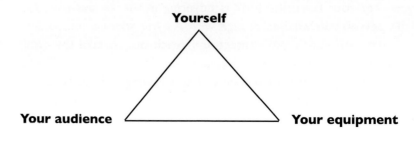

Yourself

Your audience   **Your equipment**

You need to know where you are so that you are thinking about your position relative to the audience – are you too close, too far away, too much over to one side?

You need to be aware of your audience. Are they paying attention? Is one part of the audience less involved than another – what does that mean for your gestures?

You need to be particularly aware of your equipment. A specific challenge that I always face is when I am using a laptop and a projector. I use the laptop as a visual cue to remind me of my slide. I am engaging the audience with eye contact and the audience is looking at the screen behind me. I always have to remember to point at the main screen and not at the laptop. I have seen people even go so far as to use a laser pointer on the computer screen rather than the large screen that the audience is watching.

Crocodile summary

- Hands relaxed and loose at the sides when not in use

- Hands relaxed and held gently at just above waist height when not in use

- Gestures always above the waist

- Gestures from the shoulder not the elbow

- Appropriate width of gesture for audience size

- Use asymmetry

- Stand still when communicating key points

Look Me In The Eye

The people in your audience are vital to you. It is always surprising to me to see how little of the time inexperienced presenters spend actually looking at them. Presenters look almost anywhere else – for instance:

- The floor

- The ceiling

- Their notes

- The screen

One of the ways we judge how trustworthy people are is by watching to see if they are looking at us. We hear phrases like "shifty" used to describe people who do not engage with us. As a presenter you will be most effective if you simulate the kind of eye contact that people use when talking one to one between friends. This consists of a definite steady attention on the other person alternating with short breaks where there may be no eye contact at all.

The question then is, why don't we use good eye contact? Of all the physical presenting skills, this is the one I see used least well. I think the answer is that it can feel quite threatening to have perhaps 20 people looking at you and having to look back at them. This is understandable.

Let's break it down

- Your audience will have less belief in a message delivered to the screen or the carpet than they will if they see it being delivered to a person

- Everyone in your audience likes to feel involved so you have to look at everyone

- People dislike being stared at just as much as they dislike being ignored

This leads to two challenges:

- What pattern should I use to ensure that I involve everyone?

- How long should I look at someone for?

Patterns

The secret to effectively working a room with your eyes is to look randomly from one place to another, avoiding the sweep or lighthouse effect. If you have been looking at the front left, then look next somewhere towards the back. This makes your use of eye contact more apparent to the whole group. Although the choice of where to look is random, when you are looking somewhere you must do so steadily and without allowing your eyes to flicker around.

If you have a large audience, then mentally divide them into blocks and look at a friendly face in each block. The rest will gain a sense that you are looking at them.

Timing of Eye Contact

A few years ago, I was lucky enough to work on the same platform as a nationally known politician. His role in a weekend workshop was to speak on Friday night, in Barcelona, to a group of people who had just flown in for a meeting. His after dinner speech was entitled "Life in Westminster". The room was hot and stuffy, the audience were tired after a long week and he was speaking from a position tucked away in one corner of the room. His talk was a reasonable success and everyone retired to the bar.

I didn't know anyone so I struck up a conversation with a few of my new acquaintances and was very surprised to hear them all say more or less the same thing – "That speaker was looking at me all the way through his talk – I really felt he was delivering everything for my benefit – I hope everyone else didn't feel left out". With my interest in presenting I asked the politician about his technique. He said:

> *"I never present to an audience. I have series of short one-to-one conversations with individuals."*

The answer to the question "How long should I look at someone for?" is simple. Look at them for the duration of a thought.

Many people have been taught to use three or five seconds of eye contact. Apart from being a rather rigid piece of advice, I would imagine that you have enough on your mind with the rest of your presentation without mentally counting up to five every few seconds.

So, what do I mean by a thought? Simply this. Keep your attention on one person until there is a natural break in the rhythm or subject that you are delivering. You will probably find that it corresponds quite well with your breathing pattern. This means that your shifts in eye movement will be quite natural and you will not need to count.

Confidence

The advice from my politician colleague has another benefit. One of the pressures that presenters feel is the need to try and encompass a whole room all the time. This leads to a flitting type of eye movement that never seems to settle on anyone and makes the presenter look and feel very nervous. By reframing the idea of presenting to a group into a series of one to one chats, the challenge is reduced to something we all do every day – namely speak to one person. We can all do that. The only difference is that as a presenter, you keep changing whom it is that you talk to.

Crocodile summary

- Always deliver your words looking onto someone's eyes

- Deliver for the duration of one thought or idea

- Look somewhere else in the room and do it again.

Speak to Me

People come to my workshops very concerned about how they look and about how to do a better PowerPoint presentation. They rarely volunteer that they want to make the most of their vocal technique. This always surprises me since the sounds that a presenter makes are the way in which the bulk of the message is delivered.

There are four easily controlled variables in the voice and it is essential as a presenter that you practice working with all of these. They are:

• Pitch

• Pace

• Volume

• Silence

The next section of the book deals with the first three of these and silence is discussed at the end.

The first thing to say is that the concept of "tone" is missing from this list. For me, tone is a description of the sweetness or harshness of the voice. Control of this certainly enhances any presentation but it is a skill that requires a lot of specialised practice and I have found that it is outside the normal requirement of a presenter. If you are interested I strongly recommend the work of the famous voice coach Patsy Rodenburg.

Anyhow, back to the trio of pitch, pace and volume

Take a look at this diagram.

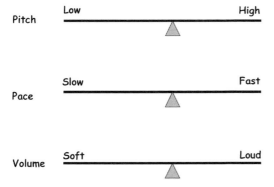

You can see here that for each of the three variables there is a range, from soft to loud, from low to high and from slow to fast. Each of us has our own personal setting along that continuum that we use in everyday conversation. This marked with the triangle on the diagram. The problem is that most people do not use much of the range on either side of that normal point. Effective presenting does have a theatrical quality to it and part of that effect is to use as much of the dynamic range as possible.

If you think about it, there is actually very little of the range that is not available to a skilful presenter.

The full range of pitch can be effective with the exception of the extreme high end of the scale. A very high-pitched voice sounds strangled and gives the impression of nervousness and panic.

The full range of pace can be used. However the extreme high-speed end of the scale should be used with caution since again it can give the impression of panic.

All of the volume scale can be used except that part which is so quiet as to be inaudible or so loud as to be shouting.

A cautionary note. The point about these scales is not to deliver a 20 minute monologue in a low pitched, slow whisper but to realise that these extremes are available to you to make a momentary impact. Much of the effective use of technique in presenting is when something changes. If you speak quite loudly and quickly as your normal style, you will grab the attention of your audience when you suddenly slow down or drop the volume of your voice.

Silence Really Is Golden...

Many people believe that they speak too quickly. In fact, I rarely come across a really rapid presenter. What people are usually doing is speaking without pausing. The human brain can keep track of information delivered much more quickly than anyone can speak. Most of us have seen or heard the famous high speed auctioneers at the cattle markets in the USA. They are speaking many times faster than normal speech but everyone there understands their message because the people listening understand the context of the message. In auditory terms they know what they are listening for.

In the context of a presentation, the difference between being understood and having a real vocal impact on the audience and not doing so, is in the silences that you use.

Silences add value to your presentation in several ways:

• They create an impression of confidence and control

• They give the audience time to consider the implications of what you have said

• They can alert the audience to an important message to follow

• They create a rhythm that, if you lose your way, gives you time to recover without revealing your momentary crisis

Silences create an impression of confidence and control because they signal to the audience that you are not afraid of interruptions. Think of the opposite. Nervous presenters gabble without pause because they are afraid that if they stop speaking, someone will ask a question that they cannot answer. Pauses say to the audience:

> "Come on – I can handle whatever you can throw at me. I'll leave a space for you to ask anything you want"

This is based on a confident frame of mind, not an arrogant one and it is a highly effective way to send a subliminal message to the audience that you know what you are doing and you are in control.

Silence is at is most effective when used in three situations within your talk

• In your introduction

• Within the flow

• When answering questions

Let's consider each of them in turn.

Unaccustomed as I am ...

It is a recurring theme in this book that the audience decides what it thinks about you very quickly, certainly well inside the one minute that is usually quoted. The first things that you do and say can shape the whole presentation. Think of two scenarios:

The presenter walks quickly and edgily into the centre of the room, and looking slightly downwards at a fixed point just in front of the first row of the audience launches into a rapid monologue.

"Good morning ladies and gentlemen, I am delighted to be here today to talk you about one of the most important developments in the field of electronics for the last ten years"

Speaking as she goes, the presenter then immediately retires to wherever the PC is located and launches into the first slide.

• Are you now looking forward to listening to this person for the next hour or so?

• Do you believe that your view on the state of the electronics industry is going to be transformed by what she is about to say?

• Do you believe that the presenter feels confident about the subject and is enjoying speaking to you?

Let's try again

The presenter walks to the centre of the room at a normal walking pace, stops and sweeping the audience briefly with a glance, smiles and nods slightly – all in silence.

Maintaining steady eye contact with the group, she speaks

"Good morning ladies and gentlemen **(pause)**

I am delighted to be here today to talk you about one of the most important developments in the field of electronics for the last ten years"

She then walks at normal pace and in silence over to where she can trigger the first slide.

How do you feel now as a member of the audience? What is it about this introduction that makes you feel calmer and more confident about what is going to happen next?

In full flow ....

Within the flow of your talk, the use of pauses is essential. When, as part of your self-development as a presenter, you invest time listening to the presentation styles of people you respect, you will almost certainly notice that they have a characteristic rhythm. Typically, the more confident a presenter is, the more pronounced are the pauses they use. Listen to various members of royal families and senior politicians and you will notice what I mean.

Over the next few weeks, try to become more aware of your natural rhythm of speech when you are talking in normal conversation. You will be most effective as a speaker if you develop your natural style into a slightly larger, more emphasised version of your normal speech patterns when you are presenting. Make sure you become aware of where you naturally pause. This is where you will use silence when you are presenting.

For a professional presenter in a business context, pauses of a count of two seconds are about right. When you practice these, literally count one-two in your mind until you get used to the pace. Two seconds is not long at all but it seems an age when you first start to use the technique. Put the pauses in at the end of each though or idea and coincide these with changing the focus of your eye contact. This will create a very natural effect.

That's a really good question ......

Pauses are an important part of the technique for answering questions because they signal that you are taking the questioner seriously. In this aspect of presenting, the biggest challenge to the speaker is not whether he knows the answer to the question, but rather preventing the answer coming back so fast that it creates the effect of dismissing or putting down the questioner.

Someone who asks you a question will want to believe that you are taking the question seriously, that you have been challenged by it and have thought about the answer. A short pause before responding achieves all of these things.

Remember these recommendations when you read the section on handling questions later in the book.

Try this:

> *Stand up and deliver these words at a level pace, pitch and volume and without pausing*
>
> *"When you get home from this workshop, if you do nothing else, remember to make full use of physical skills and voice skills such as pitch, pace and volume"*

The message you have delivered is a critical one for any presenter and yet the technique you have just used removes almost all of its impact. This delivery places total emphasis on the least important contributor to the impact – the content.

Now try it this way, paying particular attention to the bold italic notes on the left

Short pause after this phrase · *When you get home from this workshop*

Reduce your pitch pace and volume on the last 2 words so that they sound very deliberate and then pause again for 2 seconds · *If you do nothing else*

Deliver this word quite loudly and with emphasis · *Remember*

Deliver these words towards the top end of your normal range of pitch, pace and volume · *to make full use of physical skills and voice skills such as pitch, pace and volume*

This may seem quite an artificial exercise and in practice you will need to find the combinations of pitch, pace and volume that work best for you and your voice. However I am confident that when you deliver these alternatives to a friend and ask for their feedback, the second technique will have had more punch.

You may have guessed that these instructions on delivery are not random. By pausing and reducing the dynamic energy of what you are saying, you create an inconsistency. The important message is being delivered at a low energy level and this makes the audience strive to listen. You then stop talking (after "nothing else"). This momentarily opens the audience to whatever you say next and then the key message is delivered with real impact.

Remember we discussed at the beginning of the book that an audience will only recall three or so points and you have to make sure that you are in control of what those points are. The use of vocal techniques like this one are amongst the most powerful ways of achieving this objective.

Empowering Language

Presenting is about words as well as about physical techniques. One of the most effective ways of communicating confidence to the audience is to use empowering language.

Empowering language is the language of certainty. We all know its opposite very well. Have you ever heard a speaker say:

> *"Possibly, we might, perhaps be able to try and do something."*

All these words communicate uncertainty and doubt and they make the speaker seem nervous.

Speakers also often begin a talk by apologising in some way. Typical comments that reveal their uncertainty include:

* I am afraid this is quite a long talk with a great deal of detail but I will try to make it as interesting as possible

* I didn't have as much time to prepare this as I would have liked

* I haven't given a talk like this for quite a long time

So what are empowering words? Here are some examples

- I believe we will achieve something

- I am certain that this will happen

- We will definitely move forward

- I am confident that you will learn a lot from what I have to say

As for the apologies, the simple advice is don't do it. The audience usually comes to you with positive expectations and a desire to enjoy listening to you. Let them continue with their expectations and make sure that whatever you say about your talk is positive and builds on what they expect.

- I have designed this talk to be a thorough overview of the topic

- I had a week to prepare for this talk. It was great fun to be able to concentrate on just one thing and put it together over such a short time

- This is the first time I have been asked to give this talk for a while and I really enjoyed reviewing the topic and updating the material

Crocodile summary

- Make the most of variations in your pitch, pace and volume.

- Use these variations to emphasise the key points in your presentation.

- Silences give a powerful impression of control and confidence.

- Always use empowering language to build your own confidence and that of your audience.

3
I know what to do
What do I say?

Shape Up

By now you are building a solid set of presentation techniques to use to ensure that you reach your audience in the most confident, powerful and professional way possible. These techniques will work best for you when they are used within the framework of a well-designed presentation.

This section of my book takes you away from the crocodiles and back to the peace and quiet of your home or office where you can start to design the talk that you are going to deliver.

What's Going to Be Different in 20 Minutes' Time?

A presentation can only have one of a handful of objectives

*   To inform/educate

*   To change opinion

*   To entertain

*   To move people to take action

There are lots of reasons that people give me for why they actually do make presentations:

*   I was told to

*   We always have a talk on a Friday

*   The shareholders want to hear from the Managing Director

*   I am the Best Man

These are not objectives. Let's expand on them and see if they can become objectives.

- I was told to and I want to take the opportunity to look good and put myself in the running for promotion

- We always have a talk on a Friday and I want to use the time to motivate the team to support our next project

- The shareholders want to hear from the Managing Director and I want the message to reach the market that our share value is underrated by 10%

- I am the Best Man and I want the wedding guests to go away liking me and feeling they have been amused without embarrassing anyone

Now we have a goal. The majority of this book addresses the challenge of achieving the objective you set for your presentation.

What will the audience know, believe or be able to do after your presentation that they don't/can't at the moment?

There is an old acronym much beloved of salespeople. It is KISS – Keep It Short and Simple. One of the great ways to succeed as a presenter is to do the least possible to achieve your outcome and then stop talking and go home. This minimalist approach will mean that you will feel that you have the time and space to fully develop your ideas and you will find it much easier to achieve your objective within the time available. This is only possible if you have absolute certainty as to the objective you are trying to achieve. Without that clarity, most presenters adopt a shotgun approach, adding slides and information "just in case". The presentation loses direction and focus and the audience feels confused and unsatisfied.

Before you decide what you want to say, take a few minutes to consider your audience. A presentation needs to achieve the objective that you have set. The best way to achieve this objective is to present in the way that makes it easiest for your audience to understand and agree with. Stephen Covey in his book "The Seven Habits of Highly Effective People" says "Begin with the end in mind" and this is exactly what you should do.

Think about the next presentation you are going to give. Imagine that you have delivered your talk, it was a huge success and now you can relax. What will the audience be saying? How will you feel? What will you be doing to celebrate this success? Now rewind in your mind. What will you have to have done to achieve this success? Think about the environment where you are going to give the presentation. Will it be light, cool and airy or hot and crowded? Think about where you will be on the agenda. Will you be the motivational warm up artist or in the post-lunch graveyard slot? How will you have adapted your content and style to the audience to meet their level of knowledge and interest in the subject you are going to address?

Now – write the objective for the talk and start to plan.

You now probably have a much better understanding of how to approach the presentation. If you like you can take this exercise a step further to get an even better understanding.

Imagine now that you are literally a "fly on the wall" watching the presentation. How is the presenter (you) coming across to the audience? Which visuals are working well? What is the presenter doing to make sure the pace is correct? How is the presenter dealing with any potentially awkward aspects of the room or the situation?

This exercise may have seemed a little strange but it takes advantage of a curious aspect of the human mind, which is that the brain cannot tell the difference between something that has happened and something that you are imagining in detail.

I teach my delegates a universal structure for a presentation. It works for casual social talks, formal business presentations and in complex technical updates. The structure has five elements and you will see that the planning for each of these elements includes working out some of the physical techniques you are going to use as well as what you are going to say.

The elements are:

•   Attention grabber

•   Credentials

- Agenda

- Content

- Call for action

Attention Grabber

Most presentations that I see begin with the words "Good afternoon, I have come to talk to you about ….."

There are two problems with that opener. Firstly the audience has not been given a reason to be interested in your topic and secondly, they do not know why they should be interested in hearing about it from you.

This is the reason for the attention grabber and the credentials part of your presentation.

Let's take a moment to think about adult learning as opposed to the way children like to receive information.

Anyone with children, nieces or nephews will have enjoyed or endured the bedtime story where a well-known character such as Red Riding Hood wanders tediously through the woods until she comes to a cottage and then meets the big scary wolf (or crocodile). Children love this slowly revealed surprise and this structure is the one most often used by adult presenters. A great deal of information is presented which then leads up to the punch line. Unfortunately most people have long since stopped listening because they were unclear as to why they were supposed to listen and what they were going to listen out for.

Adult learning principles tell us to exploit something called Primacy and Recency. This is the simple fact that adults remember more of what they hear first and last. In addition they like to know why they are listening. A much better structure for adults to hear Red Riding Hood might be to start by saying:

> *"In a moment everyone, I am going to tell you a really scary story about a wolf. It will make you jump out of your seats so listen carefully"*

You can now tell your story, complete with walk in the woods, cottage and wolf.

At the end you might then say:

> "See – I told you it was a scary story. That will teach you to watch out for wolves in the future"

One of the most successful TV detective series was built around this principle. Most of you will know the crumpled detective played by Peter Falk in the Colombo series from the 1970's. In every episode, we know who the murderer is within the first five minutes. The fascination is watching him prove it. For many people this is much more interesting than the conventional crime thriller where the villain is slowly unveiled.

The principle of using an attention grabber exploits the concept of Primacy to create the maximum impact for your presentation.

So what makes a good attention grabber?

Most importantly it should be brief – just one or two short sentences. Any longer, the impact is lost and you will tend to deliver your presentation in the introduction, only to deliver it again later.

It should contain some element of drama. This is typically a strong statistic, some idea of the social or personal impact of the topic or a reference to some aspect of the subject that you know is of primary interest to your audience.

Attention grabbers include

- Impactful statistics

- Rhetorical questions

- Quotations

- Humour

Impactful statistics
Imagine that I am about to talk to a group of doctors about a new

medicine for a disease called Prenditt's Syndrome. This is a condition which leads to backache and which prevents sufferers sleeping properly. A typical introduction might be

> "Good afternoon. My name is Stuart Wineberg and I have come to you about Prenditt's Syndrome which causes backache and sleep loss in a significant number of people."

This is a clear, concise and utterly uninspiring way to begin my talk and will have the audience heading for the exits, or a well-earned 15 minutes snooze.

How about this instead:

> "Good afternoon. Every year, 3000 people consult their GP's having endured the insomnia and chronic pain of Prenditt's Syndrome"

This is better — it is punchy and makes the subject sound important.

Now — if I combine this with a few core presentation techniques, we have a very strong attention grabbing opener

Walk out into the centre of the stage, pause, smile and glance around then ...	Good afternoon
Take a short pace forward, then ...	Every year, 3000 people consult their GP's having endured the insomnia and chronic pain of Prenditt's Syndrome

Pause again

Rhetorical questions
A lot of people like to ask questions at the beginning of a talk as a way of engaging the audience and making the presentation more interactive. These are very well-intentioned objectives but they are also very risky. There are always three answers to any question. The answers are "Yes", "No" and complete silence. Most presenters ask a question expecting to get a particular answer and if the wrong answer, or no answer comes back then they can be in a difficult position. If you do want to ask a question make it a rhetorical one.

> "Is it any wonder that after months of pain and insomnia, over 3000 people a year consult their doctor with Prenditt's Syndrome?"

Quotations

Quotations can be very effective attention grabbers. How about this one for a presentation about presenting

> "Mark Twain said, there are two types of speakers – Those that are nervous and those that are liars"

This is sharp and to the point and has the credibility of a famous author's name behind it. It also has an element of humour.

Humour

Humour is potentially dangerous. I am often asked about this. If someone asks me whether they should introduce humour into their presentations, my response is usually that since they have asked, the answer is no. What I mean by that is that truly funny people have an instinctive sense of timing that most of us lack. I prefer to encourage people to achieve a light-hearted feel to their presentation by the use of quotations or cartoons and images. Please be aware though that just because an image is available on the internet, it does not mean that you are necessarily free to take it and use it in your talk without permission.

Credentials

Notice that I haven't introduced myself yet. I want my audience awake and paying attention before I do so.

> "My name is Stuart Wineberg and I have been closely involved for the last five years in the development of a new treatment for this debilitating condition."

This brief credentials statement reminds the audience of who I am and establishes my right to be speaking on the subject of the day.

Clearly if you have been introduced by someone then you should acknowledge the introduction and then go into the attention grabber. I would refer back to the introduction to re-establish my credentials.

Occasionally, one of my delegates will query the time taken in these additional presentation steps. If they are delivered with confidence and clarity, they add less than a minute to the presentation and they make a considerable difference to its impact.

Agenda

Now we get to the place where most people start. The agenda covers these elements:

• Duration

• Main themes

• When you would like to take questions

Duration
Adult audiences like to know how long they are going to have to sit and listen. It helps them pace their concentration and increases the chances that they will still be paying attention at the end.

Most people need a change of pace every ten minutes if not more frequently. This can be:

• Change of medium – perhaps from slides to flip chart

• Change of pace – perhaps to bring in an element of inter-action

• Change of visual impact – perhaps a cartoon slide or other visual

• Change of topic

As I have already mentioned, the golden rule of presenting is always to speak for as short a time as possible whilst still allowing you to achieve your desired outcome.

Main themes
These are the core sections of the talk. In the example of my new medicine these might be:

- The disease

- The research we carried out

- Evidence that the new medicine works safely

There are a couple of important reasons for being clear about these sections from the beginning

- Signposting

- Time chunking

Signposting is exactly what it says. It is the method you use to help your audience navigate through your talk.

It allows you to let the audience know when each section starts and begins and this will guarantee you a few vital minutes of renewed attention.

Time chunking is a powerful and simple piece of psychology. If you tell your audience that you are going to speak for 30 minutes, many of them will immediately lose concentration. For them, the idea of a 30 minute monologue is too much to endure. On the other hand if you tell them that the talk has three sections, each lasting ten minutes, it is the size of the time chunk that registers in their brain and they will probably stay with you for what they perceive to be a short time.

When you want to take questions
In the next chapter, you will find a discussion on the advantages and disadvantages of the different times you can take questions and you can then decide what you want to do for the next talk you are planning to deliver.

Just one additional tip. Always express your decision positively. Tell the audience when you will take questions, not when you don't want to take them.

So, here is the agenda for my medicine talk:

> *"My talk today consists of three main sections, an overview of Prenditt's Syndrome, a description of our work and of course an*

> *explanation of why this new medicine is such an important development in the management of the condition. Each section will last about 10 minutes and I will be delighted to take any questions as we go along. We will also have the opportunity for a more general discussion at the end."*

Content

This section is obviously up to you to design. Apart from my recommendation to be as brief as possible, also remember:

- Think about your audience. Aim to give them information that is relevant to them. If you are a genuine expert in your topic then resist the temptation to prove it using huge amounts of detail

- Use your signposts. Constantly let the audience know where they are in the flow and how much more is still to be delivered. Never apologise for the amount of time left to the end

- If you begin to run out of time, start to cut the content back to your key themes. **Always cut, never speed up**

Call for Action

Think back to when we discussed the objectives for a presentation. There are only a handful

- To inform/educate

- To change opinion
- To entertain

- To move people to take action

The call for action is simply where you remind the audience why you are speaking to them and where you ask them to do whatever it is you came there to get them to do.

Many presenters think that the logical and sequential presentation of their content means that what they want the audience to do will be obvious. Unfortunately, the audience is listening to what you say through a set of filters. These are filters that are based on their life experiences, their perspective on the topic and frankly, what happened to them that morning. All of these have the potential to lead them to interpret your message in a very different way to what you expect. In order to make sure that your message is interpreted in the way you want, you will have to be absolutely clear about it.

For my delegates, one of the most challenging aspects of structuring a presentation is to end the talk convincingly. If the need to exploit Primacy is the driver for the strong attention grabber; then Recency is the driver for a powerful close.

One of the secrets to a strong close to a talk is to discover your hidden presenter style. Presenters tend to fall into two categories that I call enthusiasts or reasonable people. To make sure you can get the most out of this section, please make sure that you take another look at the advice on voice technique and particularly remind yourself of the diagram showing the ranges of pitch, pace and volume.

Enthusiasts are naturally energetic, they tend to convince their audience by a dynamic delivery, usually towards the right hand end of the pitch, pace and volume ranges.

Reasonable people are quiet and sincere. They convince by sounding honest and well considered, usually towards the left hand side of the vocal range.

You will naturally fall into one of these groups and the trick is to use the alternative style for the final part of your presentation where you ask the audience to take action. The reason for this is that after 20 minutes or so of even the most effective style, the audience tends to be lulled by it and will lose concentration to some extent. You need your audience to be fully awake and listening to you at the point that you tell them what to do. The best way to do this is to signpost it by using a change of style.

So, if you are an enthusiast, pause for a moment and then, using a slightly slower delivery and a quiet voice ask the audience to take action.

If you are a reasonable person, step forward, increase the volume and pace and deliver your request for action with real impact.

Let me tell you a story

Your presentation should tell a story. It should draw in the people in the audience, hold them and let them feel that they are being led down a well-constructed path towards an outcome that they can understand and relate to. Many of the presentations I hear come across as jerky, unconnected snippets of information that simply aren't going anywhere. The secret to this is in the links between the snippets. The human brain is very effective at creating sense out of nonsense. It's what we do all the time to enable us to function in our complex world. Most presenters seem to think quite carefully about what they want to say in support of each PowerPoint slide they show but they don't build the links. If we continue with our new medicine, imagine that the presenter has three slides, one showing how well the drug works, one showing how safe it is and one showing how much it costs. Typically, the presentation would sound like this:

> "This slide shows how well our new medicine controls the symptoms of Prenditt's Syndrome."
>
> "This slide shows how safe our new medicine is"
>
> "This slide shows what good value for money our new medicine is"

Each of these statements is correct and is supported by an excellent PowerPoint slide but there is no story.

This is a better alternative.

> "This slide shows how well our new medicine controls the symptoms of Prenditt's Syndrome. Naturally, the real benefit of a new medicine can only be achieved if it is safe as well as effective and I want to show you the safety information in the next slide"

> *"As I said, this slide shows how safe our new medicine is. You can now see that we have both an effective and safe new treatment. In these days of increasing financial pressure, any new medicine will only be accepted if it represents good value for the patient and the hospital and that is why we have prepared some information on cost benefit for you to consider and that is on my next slide."*
>
> *"This slide shows what good value for money our new medicine is"*

You can see from this example that the links create a flow and a sense of logical progression in your story. The links should describe:

•   The connection between the topic in the current slide and the topic you want to address next. In this case that effective treatment is only useful if we also have safety

•   A description of the slide that you are about to show

Less is More

I am frequently asked how much detail to include in a presentation. On most occasions I find myself recommending less than the speaker had planned to include.

The rule is simple; say the least that is necessary to achieve your objective and then stop.

Get it off your chest

A valuable technique is to plan your presentation by downloading from your brain everything you could say during your presentation using one of the common creative thinking techniques such as brainstorming (not something to do alone) and mind mapping. There are multiple resources available for you to help with this process.

Have a look at http://en.wikipedia.org/wiki/Brainstorming or http://en.wikipedia.org/wiki/Mind_map. Once you have done this you can cut down and organise the material into a logical flow, always keeping your end objective firmly at the centre of your plan. Once you have created your presentation, sit back and ask yourself if there is any part of it that you can cut out without affecting your core message. It can be very useful to show your talk to a friend who has a similar level of interest and expertise to the audience that you will actually deliver your material to.

If you were in your audience – what would you want to know in order to agree with the content of the presentation?

Crocodile summary

- Know what your talk is meant to achieve and design everything to move towards that objective

- Follow a clear, high impact structure for your presentation

- Use signposts to help the audience keep track of where you are in the talk

- Have a clear call for action

- Tell a story

- Say the least you can in order to achieve your objective

4
I've said it
What happens next?

How Can I Help?

Whenever one of my workshops gets round to the topic of handling questions, the mood in the room changes. Everyone listens harder; people who have been a little quiet suddenly have lots they want to ask.

This isn't surprising, questions are the moment when you run the risk of handing control of your presentation to someone else and that creates the potential for pressure and the unexpected.

So, what are the important issues surrounding questions? These are the things I am often asked:

•   Are questions a good thing or bad for the presenter and
        the presentation?

•   When is the best time to take questions?

•   What is the best process for answering questions?

•   How do I encourage questions?

•   What if I don't know the answer?

•   What about troublemakers and disruptive people?

To answer the first of these points, I need you to think back to the start of the book where we discussed the reasons for delivering a presentation. Do you remember the bit about "What will be different in 20 minutes time?"

Questions are always a good thing because they allow you to restate the main points of your argument, to move the audience closer to your objective.

They are also the most important way that you can close the communication loop. The communication loop is a way of describing the overall process of communication.

Most speakers deliver only half of a message.

The presenter formulates an idea in his brain and turns it into code — the code is the words that he speaks and the images that he shows on the screen.

Each person in the audience receives the code and translates it back into thoughts using the unique method that each individual has developed based on their genetics and life experiences. This is often described as their "rose tinted spectacles".

Message transmitted		Changed message received

Message filtered, distorted and deleted

At this point the speaker has no idea what thoughts the presentation has generated.

It is only when a member of the audience speaks — usually by asking questions — that the speaker begins to understand what thoughts have been generated in the mind of the questioner and the loop is completed.

It is essential that you close the communication loop in every presentation that you deliver — either by generating questions or by starting a discussion — something we will examine later in this chapter.

The only exception to this rule is a presentation designed entirely to entertain. Hopefully you will have closed the communication loop through the loud and appreciative laughter that you will have heard during the talk.

Timing is very important in a presentation.

Encouraging and answering questions is an essential part of any professional presentation

A vital part of that timing is when to take questions. Your options are clearly either during the presentation or at the end. There are no hard and fast rules for this but it is worth considering some of the pros and cons:

During – pros	During – cons
The issue is addressed at the moment that it is important to the questioner	You might be going to address the issue later anyway
You receive immediate feedback as to whether you are delivering at the right level or on the right topic	The questions eat into your time in an unpredictable way
	Your thought processes and flow can be disrupted
After – pros	**After – cons**
You can deliver your full message exactly in the way that you planned	Someone trying to remember a question for later may not listen to the rest of your talk
Time management is easier	You may have missed a key issue that the question would have revealed if delivered earlier

Overall, if you are confident of your subject and your audience and feel fully in control, then take questions as you go along. It comes across as more professional and it deals with issues as they arise.

If you are in any way unsure or if the material is new to you, then take questions at the end to give you more control.

Don't forget that people in the audience may well ignore your request and ask the questions any time they like. Always be prepared for this to happen and decide whether to insist on your rules or be flexible. You can always take the question and if you are going to address it later, then say so.

What is the best process for answering questions?

There are two answers to this. One is to use a core question answering flow to deal with the issue in a confident and professional way. This keeps you on the topic set by the questioner. The other, and more sophisticated way is to first of all consider what issue you want to deal with before you answer. The next section of the book deals with both of these in turn but firstly we need to go into the mind of the questioner.

Why **do** people ask questions?

There are several answers to this and only one of them is to gain additional information. Other reasons are:

• To express their own opinion

• To look good in front of their peers

In many situations, delivering a presentation is part of a larger communi-cation strategy. It might be part of a complex sales process or perhaps part of a programme to motivate a group of people to join a society or to contribute to a charitable cause. In these situations it is important to avoid winning a battle and losing the war.

In other words, a slick pointed answer to a question can alienate a potential ally in your achievement of the larger objective.

In nearly every case, if the questioner is asking a question to look good or to impress others, then help them do so.

With this objective in mind we can now develop a method for answering questions.

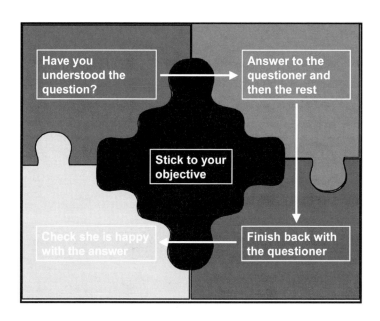

Have you understood the question?

→ Answer to the questioner and then the rest

Stick to your objective

Check she is happy with the answer

← Finish back with the questioner

A good answer to a question is one that helps you achieve your objective and also helps the questioner achieve theirs

This flow starts with the thought – do I know what I am being asked? It is all too easy to assume that the person asking the question has uncovered some fundamental flaw in our argument. The danger is that we then jump into a long defensive answer which just reveals all too clearly the flaw we were trying to conceal.

Strangely it is the short questions that are the biggest hazard. If someone asks a long question, they are usually quite precise.

Let's assume you are singing the praises of a new model of motorbike.

> *"If I change into second gear on this motorcycle, how quickly can I accelerate to 70mph?"*

There is really only one answer to this question.

How about this one?

> *"How does it perform?"*

This could mean all sorts of things

- What is the 0-100 acceleration time?

- What is the fuel consumption?

- Does it handle well on wet roads?

- Is it stable in a cross wind?

With a vague, short question like this you need to do two things

- Make the questioner feel it was a worthwhile question to ask

This is best done with a combination of verbal and non-verbal behaviour.

- Find out what they really want to know

So – take a step towards the person and look interested.

He feels important and that he has asked a good question	"Thanks for that question – performance is definitely an important topic for a bike like this one"
This is called a point question – it takes a broad issue and demands a narrow, directed answer	"Tell me – what specific aspect of performance were you particularly interested in?"

You now gain thinking time. There is a risk that the questioner may be confused by your point question since he may not know what aspect of performance he is interested in. Be prepared to rescue him.

> "I am often asked about the performance of this bike in wet weather……."

Now you know what information is required, you can begin to answer. Start off by doing so directly to the questioner but after one thought or idea, broaden out to deliver the answer to the whole audience. As you finish the answer refocus your attention onto the original questioner.

Make sure he is satisfied with your answer. This does not mean asking if he agrees – he will often reply no to this one, and you will have to start the whole process again. A simple nod, an "OK", and a smile will usually suffice.

Finally – always remember that the whole question answering process is there to help you achieve your objective. Be polite but give little time to irrelevant questions, expand and amplify your answers to ones that can be made to reinforce your key messages.

This method is a highly effective approach to giving a straightforward, controlled and professional answer to a question. It has only one limitation and that is that the questioner is controlling the topic. Because of this I have developed a more sophisticated technique, which is similar to that used by politicians. I call it the "no-lose technique".

No-Lose Technique

In any presentation there will be elements of the content that you would like to emphasise and others that you would like to minimise. Nonetheless, in the interests of honesty, you have to give truthful answers. The no-lose technique allows you to open up the topic until it is sufficiently broad to allow you to talk about your objectives as well as deal concisely with the question that was asked.

Let's consider another scenario:

You are representing a charitable organisation. You do good deeds all over the world but because of the very complicated situations where you work, your administrative costs are a little higher than most other charities. This is easily offset by the high level of skill that you bring to disaster hit and deprived parts of the world.

Your objective for the presentation is to emphasise the scope and quality of the charitable work that you carry out.

If you are asked, "Aren't your administrative costs excessively high?" the temptation is to talk at length about the administrative structure of your charity, showing relevant data and so on. This becomes a good answer on the wrong topic. You want to be talking about the good work that you do.

A better way is to follow this flow:

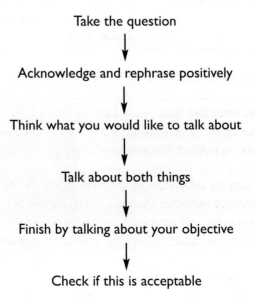

Take the question

↓

Acknowledge and rephrase positively

↓

Think what you would like to talk about

↓

Talk about both things

↓

Finish by talking about your objective

↓

Check if this is acceptable

In this example the flow would be

Aren't your administrative costs extremely high?

> *"Thank you. If I understand you, you would like to be sure that we give our donors good value for money"*

Notice my shift in the description of the issue. The questioner has asked about high administrative costs, I have rephrased the question into one about "value for money".

This is a fundamental and very important technique. The human brain cannot imagine the lack of something. So if I say that our administrative expenses are not high, the idea of expense is associated strongly with me even though I was suggesting it was NOT an issue.

Other examples of this include:

Questioner	Paraphrase
This looks dangerous	This questioner wants to be sure this is safe
This will never work	The questioner wants us to be sure it will work
We will never get approval	Important issue – we need to be sure we can get approval – let's discuss how

Remember - I want to talk about our good work

> *"This is an important issue – the balance between the scope and importance of the work done by a charity has to be balanced by what it costs to achieve that outcome"*
>
> *"It is true that our administrative costs are slightly higher than is the case for most conventional charities, however these are more than offset by the range and complexity of the challenges we face, which would not even be considered by most charitable foundations."*
>
> *"Does this answer your question?"*

Cautionary note: It takes practice to use this technique well. Practice your answers to typical questions before the event. You almost certainly know what it is the audience is likely to ask you.

So why do I call this the "no-lose" technique? The reason is simple – you are 100% certain to be closer to your objective after using this technique than if you had not done so. Think about it. Most of the time, the audience will be completely happy with your answer, which has expanded and broadened out the scope of the discussion. Very rarely, the questioner will come back at you and you will have to give a more direct answer. In this case you have to discuss your costs but only after you have re-emphasised the key point of your talk; the good works that you do. So whatever happens you are a winner.

If you are asked a question that is a complete surprise then I recommend that you answer it using the core technique described at the beginning of this section. Make a note of the question and when you get home, have a coffee and think about the optimal answer using the "no-lose" method. You now have a new weapon in your armoury for next time.

All of this assumes that someone has asked a question and I recommend several excellent techniques to increase the chances of this happening.

Any questions???

This is the commonest way most people try to get someone to ask a question. It contains within it the deep-seated hope that no-one will do so. Anyone reading this who has ever been in a sales role will recognise that it is a closed question, inviting a "yes" or "no" answer. Since a "no" answer will close the issue and move to the lunch break without any further delay and a "yes" answer will require thought and take time, it is not surprising that silence often follows.

The secret is to manage the audience's expectations at the beginning of the talk. Begin by telling the listeners that they will have some questions. Something like:

> *"This is a subject that most audiences find fascinating and I am sure you will have lots of questions which I will be happy to answer at the end"*

This piece of subtle influence tells the audience several things:

- That you are an experienced presenter since you have delivered this talk to other audiences

- That the talk is fascinating and so they should expect to find it fascinating as well

- That they will have questions and therefore they should listen and concentrate

- That you are in control and will take questions at the end

Not a bad outcome for less than thirty words.

When you get to the end of your talk, turn off the projector, stand in the centre of the stage, pause a moment, smile and refer back to your introduction:

> *"As I mentioned at the beginning, I am sure you will have lots of questions and I will be delighted to take the first one now"*

Once again, these few words exert a considerable influence:

- The audience is reminded that they were supposed to have been planning questions

- The language is very positive and encourages a response, especially the use of the word "sure"

- You mention the "first one", suggesting that there should be more than one

None of these techniques carries a certainty of success but in most cases you will get a response. If not, move to phase 2.

Phase 2 is the simple technique of asking yourself a question

> *"While you are thinking of the first question, something I am often asked about is ...."*

This technique, much used by conference Chairpeople, has the advantage that, since you are asking the question of yourself, it is quite likely that you know the answer; at least I hope so.

Phase 3 is to ask someone in the audience a question. This requires you to know the audience reasonably well since you need to approach someone who will be confident enough to respond. The other important point here is always to ask the person a question of opinion, never of fact. Think about the situation. You are an important person, sitting in front of your staff and you are asked a factual question. In the surprise and pressure of the moment, your mind goes blank and you cannot answer. It is safe to assume you would be very angry and would seek revenge on the questioner at a suitable later point. On the other hand, it is always possible to create some sort of an answer when asked for an opinion.

From your point of view as the presenter, it does not matter as long as the dialogue between you and your audience has begun.

Finally, what happens if you do not know the answer to the question? This is a fear that many of my delegates express and the first thing to say is that it happens a lot less frequently than you might imagine.

*   You are speaking on a topic that you know something about; otherwise you would not be there

*   You have researched the topic and practiced your talk

*   You have thought about what the audience might ask and for each of these possible questions you have prepared a reasonable answer

We are really dealing here with fear of the unknown and the first step is to deal with the fear itself. If you do not know the answer then potentially you are in some difficulty. You have two choices – to be in some difficulty and be unhappy about it or to be in some difficulty and be cheerful about it. This is absolutely your choice and I recommend you choose the latter.

What this means in practice is that a question to which you do not know the answer is an opportunity to learn something and that is always good news. So smile, breathe out gently and take a step towards the questioner. All of these will give a powerful impression of confidence and mean that even if you do not answer the question, you will still be perceived as a strong, controlled presenter.

Next, make sure you achieve the key objective of making the questioner

If this is a topic of particular interest to you then you might want to jump ahead to Chapter 7 where I discuss techniques for building your confidence as a presenter.

feel good about having asked a searching question and at the same time make sure you understand it.

> *"That's a very interesting point which I hadn't considered before. Tell me, what leads you to ask that?"*

Very often, the supplementary information they give will allow you to realise what the answer should be, or at least understand the motivation behind the question.

You now have several options

> *"I haven't been asked that before and I don't know the answer. I will find out and get back to you. Can I take your contact details at the end?"*

This is the most common approach to use but with a couple of positive twists. You are telling the questioner that she has thought of a question that no-one has ever thought of before. This builds rapport and makes what you say next much less important. The request for their contact details confirms that you are serious about getting back to them and not just giving them a brush-off.

Or you can say

> *"That's an interesting point. What does everyone else think?"*

This gives you access to the combined experience of the whole audience, gives you thinking time and gives you a temporary delay in having to admit that you do not know the answer. It may also give someone in the audience a chance to look good. Most importantly it makes you look a lot less exposed. If the whole audience doesn't know then it is not surprising that you do not either.

Troublemakers

Firstly, please realise that these people are relatively rare. In typical business presentations or in talks to local societies the audience will almost always be on your side.

Troublemakers fall into three categories

- Seekers for the truth

- Attention seekers

- People with a vested interest in opposing you

Seekers for the truth
These are the people who ask what seem to be very negative questions but who are in fact just detail orientated people. This type of person needs to be sure he has understood you and that you have thought through your own argument. You will see these people described in the section on "theorists" later in this chapter.

Treat these people positively, look for the real message in what they are asking and welcome the fact that if convinced, they will probably be very committed supporters of your idea.

Attention seekers
Again, we have discussed these people already. They are by far the most common troublemakers. As you have read, the easiest way to deal with them is to help them achieve their objective: in other words to make them look good in front of the audience. Your only challenge is to make sure that in so doing you do not let them monopolise proceedings. A useful phrase after answering their question is:

> *"Thank you for that question. I would like to broaden the discussion out a little – who else would like to ask me something?"*

People with a vested interest in opposing you
You will almost certainly know in advance if you are going to meet someone like this. If you are presenting on a contentious issue that has definite opponents then expect that someone like this might appear.

Situations might be:

- Where you are objecting to a building development and you know the developer is going to be at the meeting

- Where you are speaking in support of a subject when you know that a long-standing advocate of the opposing view will be there

- When you are making a proposal to have a service outsourced to your organisation and the current in-house manager will be there

The first step in handling these situations is research and preparation. Find out what the person is like, what is their general style in meetings, what arguments do they tend to put across. Then prepare.

You will probably not make them happy with your answers and you will not change their point of view. They are not there to be convinced or happy, they are using your presentation as a platform to make their point. Follow this process:

- Let them make their point

- Ignore any personal attacks — be careful not to respond sarcastically

- Respond to any factual information

- Insist on the last word. This is the most important point. If they keep interrupting, appeal to the chairman if there is one or simply say something like:

> "I have been invited to make a proposal and I am always happy to hear other points of view. I would appreciate the same courtesy in being allowed to make my point as I have given to those audience members who wanted to ask questions."

Questions are a wonderful way of saying what you want to say. Listen carefully for the opportunity to use them as a springboard back to your core messages. In truth, you will know what most of the questions are going to be. Prepare your answers and deliver them with confidence.

Crocodile summary

- Encouraging and handling questions is an essential part of any presentation.

- Make sure you achieve your objective whilst helping the questioner to achieve his or hers.

- Make sure that your answer supports your overall objective for the presentation.

- Most troublemakers are actually not trying to be difficult — it's just the way they express their questions.

Facilitating Discussion

The most usual thing that happens at the end of a presentation is a short question and answer session. In many situations, it would be more productive to start a discussion instead.

A discussion is simply an interchange between members of the audience. Although you will control it to some extent, you do not need to be the focal point of that interchange. In fact it can be very useful to try to pull back from the debate and listen.

Discussions have a number of advantages:

- The people involved tend to forget you are there and usually begin to speak in a less guarded way

- You are no longer the focus of attention and so you can take a breather

- More people become involved than would do so in a question and answer session

- You have the chance to observe and find out who your allies are (or otherwise)

Physical techniques

Everything that you have read in this book will support you in delivering a powerful and authoritative presentation. You are in control, you are highly visible and you are the complete focus of attention. These are also the techniques that will tend to prevent your audience easily transitioning into a discussion.

When you reach the end of a talk and when you want to start a discussion you should send out some strong body language signals that the mood has changed. These can include:

*   Move your weight onto one hip to look more relaxed

*   Sit on the edge of the table and open your hands as if to say "over to you"

*   Sit down

You can also direct the audience verbally

> *"Ladies and Gentlemen — you have heard what I have to say — where do we go from here?"*
>
> *"This is a situation some of you must have faced — what was your approach to managing it?"*
>
> *"We have 10 minutes left — it would be very interesting to hear your point of view"*

Once the conversation begins and starts to develop a momentum without your input, switch your attention to listening and evaluating what is going on.

So far, so good. Everyone is discussing what a wonderful person you are and how interesting your topic is and how much they agree with you.

Then you hear a voice of dissent

> *"I'm not sure about this — I can think of a few problems with this proposition"*

It is now time to reassert control. Don't rush, but stand up and resume the powerful central position. In most cases the discussion will fade away and the audience will look at you. If things are getting too lively you may have to draw things to a close. Always do this in a way that is perceived to benefit the audience rather than you.

> *"Ladies and gentlemen, this has been a very interesting discussion. However I know that you are rather pressed for time so we should bring it to a close"*

You are back in control but you still have a problem. The human brain remembers best what it heard first and last. You have just halted the discussion because of some negative comments and these are still firmly embedded in the minds of your audience.

It is essential that you close the communication loop by exerting your right as the speaker/chair. This is the right to summarise and have the last word.

> *"Before we close, ladies and gentlemen I would like to thank you for your very active contribution. We have covered a lot of ground and several key points have been made. For me the most important of these are ………"*

You now summarise the key points that are the reason for you being here – the three key objectives that are the purpose of your presentation.

Crocodile summary

•   Use physical techniques to encourage discussion

•   Keep a low profile as long as the topic is supporting your objective

•   Reassert control if the direction of the conversation changes

•   Always have the last word

Who are these people anyway?

It is likely that you have been on the receiving end of several presentations over the years. Some of them seemed excellent; some of them were probably terrible. It is worth spending a few minutes thinking about what it was that created that impression in your mind.

Whatever it was that you liked, part of it will almost certainly have been that the presenter was delivering the information or other content in a way that suited your personal learning style.

Peter Honey and Alan Mumford developed their learning styles theory from the work of David Kolb. Using their theory, the world is divided into

•   Activists

•   Reflectors

•   Theorists

•   Pragmatists

I'll expand on these in a moment but you may be asking what this has to do with delivering an effective presentation? The simple answer is that it is very likely that you will tend to write and deliver your presentations in a way that makes sense to you and in a way that you would respond to if you were in the audience. This is a perfectly reasonable thing to do. Unfortunately, a significant proportion of the population takes on information and learns in a different way to you.

Let's take a look at these categories and see what I mean.

Activists

•   Involve themselves fully and without bias, in new experiences

•   Enjoy the here and now and are happy to be dominated by immediate experiences

•   Are open-minded, not sceptical and this tends to make them enthusiastic about everything new

•   Their philosophy is: "I'll try anything once". They tend to act first and consider the consequences afterwards

•   Their days are filled with activity, they tackle problems by brainstorming

•   Are gregarious people constantly involving themselves with others but, in doing so, they seek to centre all activities on themselves

You can see that the activists in your audience will want to get out and put your ideas into action. They want to know how your ideas will improve their lives today. They are classic "big picture" people, impatient with detail and with a dislike of sitting listening to lots of long explanations. They are going to appreciate a short, punchy talk with the benefits made very clear from the onset.

Reflectors

- Like to stand back to ponder experiences and observe them from many different perspectives

- The thorough collection and analysis of data about experiences and events is what counts, so they tend to postpone reaching definitive conclusions for as long as possible

- Their philosophy is to be cautious

- Prefer to take a back seat in meetings and discussions

- Listen to others and get the drift of the discussion before making their own point

- Tend to adopt a low profile and have a slightly distant, unruffled air about them

- When they act, it is part of a wide picture which includes the past as well as the present and other peoples' observation as well as their own

The reflectors in the audience want to take their time. They are suspicious of huge levels of energy in a speaker. They tend to think that this is some sort of a smoke screen to hide weak information or a poor idea. They need to be given space to absorb your ideas before being asked to do anything. With this kind of audience the "call for action" can most effectively be to ask them to consider what you have said carefully and then to act. The reflectors in an audience often have questions in their mind that they do not ask and you may have to suggest typical areas of additional information they might be interested in.

Theorist

- Adapt and integrate observations into complex but logically sound theories

- Think problems through in a vertical, step-by-step, logical way

- Build a wide range of facts into coherent theories

- Tend to be perfectionists who won't rest easy until things are tidy and fit into a rational scheme

- Like to analyse and synthesise

- Are keen on basic assumptions, principles, theories, models and systematic thinking

- Their philosophy values rationality and logic

- Questions they frequently ask are: "Does it make sense?", "How does this fit with that?", "What are the basic assumptions?"

Theorists need a well-structured, logical argument that fits into a well-defined framework. For example, the idea that there are four learning styles that can be recognised and require differing approaches is something that would naturally appeal to a theorist. They can be very challenging people to deal with. They ask many questions and because they are testing your theory or proposition, they can come across as rather negative. We have already discussed theorists as the "seekers for the truth" earlier in this chapter.

A theorist would typically express a question something like:

> *"Ah but that would never work because of xxxxx"*

The key to remaining confident and positive when dealing with theorists is to recognise the good intention behind their searching questions. They want to accept your ideas and they want to use them. However they can only do this if the ideas have survived a rigorous challenge. Once they are satisfied, they can become your most committed allies.

Pragmatists

- Are keen on trying out ideas, theories and techniques to see if they work in practice

- Positively search out new ideas and take the first opportunity to experiment

- Are the sort of people who return from a course brimming with new ideas that they want to try out in practice

- Like to get on with things and act quickly and confidently on ideas

- Are impatient with extensive discussion

Pragmatists frankly don't care why something works or why something is a good idea. Their measure is whether it works in practice. They get bored very quickly and your main objective with them should be to get them to go and put your proposal into action as soon as possible.

You are probably asking yourself two questions by now. One is – what is my learning style? The other is how do I design my presentation when most audiences will contain people with a range of learning styles?

You probably have a sense of your preferred style just from reading the descriptions but to obtain your profile you can go to www.peterhoney.com where the questionnaire is available on a pay as you go basis.

The other question is a little trickier. At any moment, however effective your presenting style, you will be appealing to one of the learning styles more than the others. The good news is that people are very tolerant of other styles as long as they know that their needs are being acknowledged. For instance, here is a way of keeping the pragmatists and activists at bay whilst giving enough information for the theorists.

> *"Some of you, I know, would like to hear more detail about how we arrived at our conclusions. This will take me about five minutes and then I will go straight on to look at the practical approaches we have used in putting these ideas into action".*

Notice a couple of things.

Firstly the use of signposting – explaining how long the detailed explanation will take.

Secondly – the absence of any sort of apology for taking those extra five minutes.

You will perceive the rest of the world from your own position. If you are a theorist – then just about everyone will seem superficial to you. If you are a pragmatist, most people will seem bogged down in detail. Remember you are presenting in order to achieve your objective. If that means delivering a level of detail that is more or less than you would personally prefer then just do it and enjoy the freedom that having a flexible and adaptable delivery style will give you.

Crocodile summary

*   Deliver your presentation with your audience in mind

*   Deliver in a way that will enable them to agree with your proposition with the least effort on their part

*   Work to meet the needs of different styles of people throughout your presentation

5
Special situations

I just wanted to say a word .....

One of the topics in the spectrum of speaking in public that causes the most concern is being asked to say a few words at very short notice. Most of the people I meet like to plan and prepare, a feeling that is easy to understand.

So, you are sitting quietly in your office, a head comes around the door and a colleague says, "Joan is leaving today and we are making the presentation in half an hour, can you come and say a few words?" I am assuming that since your colleague has asked you to make this speech, you know something about Joan and she would expect you to be the one speaking.

After the initial sinking feeling and sense of panic, you realise that you need to move pretty quickly. Don't. Reach for a pad and pen and just like any other presentation, start with the objective. Here are a few you might consider:

- Make Joan look good

- Make sure Joan leaves the building with warm and positive memories of her time with the Company

- Come across as positive, in control and someone with the authority to tell Joan what the organisation thinks about her

Be brief, positive and to the point

The secret of the off the cuff presentation is brevity. You need to be totally focused on the impression you create. Any information that you give is secondary although it does need to be accurate – for instance when Joan joined the Company.

Here's that off the cuff speech:

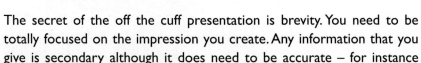

All of this is content free and obvious but also very positive and personal

It is both a pleasure and a sadness for me to be asked to say a few words today as Joan leaves us. It is a pleasure because I want to take the opportunity to give my personal best wishes as well as convey the best wishes of everyone in the organisation. It is a sadness because we are losing one of our longest serving and most valued members of the team.

If you can, a quick call to HR will get the accurate dates. Notice the mild humorous comment is at my expense not hers. Never say anything even vaguely negative abut the person on these occasions unless you want to risk tears

We all know that Joan has given us long and valuable service, but you may not know that Joan actually joined us something over 30 years ago and she is one of the few people in the organisation to have given such a length of long and uninterrupted service. In comparison, my 15 years seems quite meagre.

Make reference to whatever it is that the person values as their unique contribution. In this case Joan likes to organise her managers. Always imply that no-one will quite do it as well as the person who is leaving

Joan, I am sure that people have spoken to you individually and expressed their regrets that you are leaving and I want to add my voice to those. I will particularly miss the sense of order you have brought to the chaos of what we do on a day to day basis. I know my in-tray will never be completely tidy again.

I know that you are planning to spend more time with your grandchildren who I am sure will be easier to control than we are and I would ask everyone to join me in wishing you a very long, happy and healthy retirement.

Other situations where you may have to do this sort of quick talk will be:

•   Vote of thanks to a guest speaker

•   Introducing a guest speaker

In truth, you should have some advance notice of these. The challenge with the vote of thanks speech is that it has to link to what the speaker has said and you do not know what that is going to be in advance.

In these cases:

*   Just talk about the positive things

*   Say what it meant to you personally

*   If possible mention where you have experienced whatever it is the speaker has been talking about

*   Say what you believe it will mean to the whole group

*   Mention their evident interest in and commitment to the subject. (A good comment if the speaker has gone into appalling levels of boring detail)

*   Thank them for taking the time to come to see the group

*   Ask for a round of applause

Crocodile summary

*   Off the cuff speaking is rarely completely unplanned

*   The more spontaneous it has to be, the shorter it should be

*   Be clear about your objective

Informal vs formal situations

Most of this book is aimed at increasing your ability to deliver a presentation with authority and a degree of power and control. The reason for this is that most people have some experience in delivering what I call a stand up chat but less experience of the more authoritative style.

Before you plan your presentation, you need to decide what sort of atmosphere you need to create and what the expectations of your audience will be.

- Are you speaking from the perspective of an expert with an audience that is there to learn from you?

- Are you there to try and convince the audience to follow your advice?

- Are you there to entertain and endear yourself to the audience?

- Are you there to generate debate and find out the views of the audience?

The answer to these questions will determine what style you use for your talk. So what is the difference?

The formality or otherwise of a presentation is dictated by several different considerations:

- Room layout

- How you introduce the event

- How you use your physical skills

- The media that you use

- The degree of interaction that you generate

Room layout

The most informal layout is either a simple semicircle of chairs, or, if you want to provide writing surfaces, the use of "islands" scattered round the room, much like tables in a restaurant.

Facilitators who want to be able to move around the group tend to favour an open U shape layout. At the most formal end of the spectrum are the classic classroom and theatre styles.

How you introduce the event

I always advise my delegates to manage the expectations of the audience at the beginning of the event. You will remember that part of the agenda is to specify when you want to take questions. You can also make it clear that you would like the meeting to be interactive, that you are seeking the audience's opinion and so on.

The media that you use

Some media inhibit audience involvement. If you want to guarantee an easy ride, turn off the lights and show lots of text based PowerPoint slides accompanied by your disembodied voice. You may have an easy time but I promise that nothing much will have changed after your presentation.

Flip charts or electronic whiteboards are the most interactive of media, especially when you use them to capture feedback from your audience. It is a very effective technique to use lots of flip chart sheets and gradually to cover the walls of the room with them. It creates a very personal space for the audience and real sense of involvement and interactivity. Detailed advice on facilitation is beyond the scope of this book, however it is important to use the best colours of marker pen. Avoid pastel or fluorescent colours, they are not visible at a distance. Black, blue, green and then red are the commonest colours in their descending order of visibility.

The degree of Interaction that you generate

The focus of this book is the delivery of a presentation to an audience who are invited to ask questions either during or after the talk. This is only one method on a continuum that runs all the way through to fully interactive training where there may be very little direct input from the front. Here are some ideas that will give you an insight into your options for reducing formality and increasing interaction.

Post-presentation discussion
This technique should be part of your standard repertoire as a presenter and you have already read about generating discussion as a specific topic in the previous chapter.

Flip Chart Facilitation

This is a way for you to capture the opinions of the group without making someone stand up and present to you all. You pose a question to the audience and gather the ideas onto a flip chart. This gives you a real insight into the feelings of the group.

You should use this technique where you feel very confident of your subject, as you will have to respond to what the audience says.

Post-It Facilitation

This is a variation on the previous method. It has the advantage of giving you a breather and not requiring you to write everything down. In this method you give everyone a pad of Post-It stickers, pose a question to the group and ask them to write their responses, one per Post-It sheet. For instance here is one I use at the start of my Train the Trainer workshop.

> *"You have all been trained or taught at some time in your lives. Some of this was excellent, some of it was probably truly terrible. Please write down what was good about the best training you have received and what was bad about the worst – one idea per Post- It sheet and then come and stick your ideas up on the flip chart. The chart with the smiley face is for the good ideas, the sad face is for the bad ones."*

It usually takes about 10 minutes for people to respond fully to this and I make a judgment based on the number of delegates as to whether to get them to do this alone or in pairs or threes. People generally come up with better ideas if they are working with someone else.

Syndicates

Syndicate sessions are where you break your audience up into smaller groups and allocate to each group a topic to discuss and then to feed back to the whole audience for open discussion. It can be the same topic for everyone or different ones for each syndicate. This is a very useful technique if you have a large audience.

Audience size makes a big difference to the group dynamics. Anything under about six and there aren't enough people to generate any real interaction and energy. Over about 12 and it becomes rather intimidating for someone to offer an opinion or ask a question. The larger the audience, the more likely it is that you will be delivering a monologue. The optimum size of group for interaction is about eight and this should be your target size for a syndicate – certainly try not to drop below 4–6.

On the principle that adults dislike surprises, make it clear to your audience that you will be running one or more syndicate sessions to give them time to get used to the idea. Remember to tell the syndicates to allocate:

- A chairperson

- A timekeeper

- A presenter

Ultimately you have a wide range of options open to you as to the degree of interaction and the degree of formality that you want to generate. My advice is always to spend a few minutes and consider your options rather than go into autopilot and use the technique that you used last time just because it is the first method that occurs to you.

Crocodile summary

- You can control the level of formality and the amount of interaction that takes place in your presentation

- Your objective will guide you as to what approach to use

All the world's a stage

Most of the readers of this book will be planning to deliver presentations to small to medium sized audiences in rooms lit by daylight and without microphones. There is another scale of presentation where the audience may number hundreds and the venues may be truly huge.

This section is designed for people wanting to make the most of the opportunity to present their ideas to very large groups.

All presenting is a balance between the real world and the world of the theatrical. The larger the audience and the larger the venue, the more the balance swings towards theatre.

Some general advice first of all.

Any significantly sized event will have the support of professional audio-visual staff. These are usually found either behind the projection screen or at the back of the room operating some sort of mixing desk. There is a general tradition that they are dressed in black and since they spend all night setting up the venue for you to use the next day they are also usually bleary eyed and drinking very strong coffee.

Try and arrive early enough to have a chat to them about how you are planning to deliver your presentation, whether you prefer to be behind the podium or out in front and get their general input about how every-thing works. They appreciate being consulted and can be very helpful. They will also help you fit your radio microphone if you are using one.

In an ideal world have a full rehearsal. Project every slide and say every word, check your timing, make sure the hardware works and that you understand how to use it.

You are unlikely to be using your own computer to drive the slides so bring the presentation along on a CDROM or a memory stick and be prepared to hand it over. Check in advance if there is a unified look and feel for the event. If there is, either ask the organisers for a slide template or hand over your slides in a simple black and white form and ask the technicians to format the visuals to the required style. If you do hand them over, insist on seeing the final slides well before the event so you can comment on layout and transitions.

There are some very specific gremlins that can appear, especially with the latest versions of PowerPoint. Bullet lists can automatically resize text to fit on the screen. This can lead to different font sizes from one slide to the next. Text colours and fonts can also change when converting from one background to another.

You may well be videoed during your presentation. A full discussion of media technique is beyond the scope of this book but there is one simple rule. Ignore the camera. Continue to present to the audience, keep your voice the same and keep the gestures the same. The cameraman will make adjustments – you do not need to.

So what are the challenges?

People coming away from their first large-scale presentation usually make these comments:

- I didn't know you couldn't see the audience

- My voice sounded really strange coming back through the loudspeakers

- I felt trapped behind the podium

- The screen was so huge and so close, I couldn't see my own slides

The purpose of the audio, video and lighting arrangements in a large venue is to allow each individual audience member to clearly hear, see and experience your live presentation. Everything you know about the use of your voice, your gestures and the structure of your presentation applies regardless of the venue. Let's take those speaker comments and try to understand what they tell us about the event and how it all works.

I didn't know you couldn't see the audience

Stage lighting is extremely bright and extremely hot. This is so that the light shining on you is similar in colour to daylight. The effect of stage lighting is to block out your view of the main part of the audience – all you can see is whiteness and possibly the feet of the front row of people.

Act as if you can see the audience – even if you can't

The trick is to act as if you can still see them. A great deal of money has been spent in creating the stage and the overall look of the event. If you shade your eyes with your hand, squint into the audience and comment that you can't see anyone you are destroying the theatrical illusion that so much time and effort has been invested in creating.

A better way of dealing with the lights begins before you come onto the stage. Take a look at the audience layout – how far to the sides are they sitting, how far back? If you want to build a bridge to an individual – where is that person sitting? As you walk up to the podium and the heat hits you, look out into the glare in the direction of where the audience is. Try to keep the muscles in your face relaxed. If you haven't heard the sound of stampeding feet, there is every chance that the people are still there, even if you can't see them. Use eye contact technique exactly as you would normally do in a smaller venue. The difference is that the audience position is in your mind – look for one thought towards the back left, then to the front centre etc. Gesture out into the audience. Remember that your gestures will need to be quite large to encompass such a large group of people.

You may want to run a question and answer session after your talk. If so, warn the technical team that this is going to happen and agree how the lighting will work. Usually, the room lights (called house lights) will be switched on so that you can see the audience and the lighting level on you will be reduced but not removed completely. You may switch from the podium microphones to a radio microphone or perhaps move across the stage to a chair and table that has another microphone ready for you.

My voice sounded really strange coming back through the loudspeakers

This is a reason to try and get to the venue early enough to have a quick practice session on stage. You should find out how your voice sounds through the loudspeakers. Remember that if you do this in an empty room, when the audience is in place there will be much less echo and your voice will be absorbed so it will travel less well. For an audience of more than about 50 people always use a microphone if it is offered.

The secret to effective use of microphones is to ignore them as much as possible. The type of microphone used for presenters will pick up your voice over quite a large distance. If you speak forcibly and directly into it, it will distort and add all sorts of breathing and popping noises to your speech. Present your words out into the audience, using normal voice projection and let the technician sort out the sound levels.

Ignore the microphone – project your voice normally

A common horror story is to listen as the speaker, surprised by the sound of his own voice, lowers the volume of speech. The technician responds by lifting the volume. This creates a vicious circle, which ends with a screech of feedback.

I felt trapped behind the podium

This can be a real problem. As you will discover if we meet, I am a little below average height and so when I deliver from behind a podium, I tend to disappear. We have a tradition of making a feature of this and I have often been preceded onto the stage by someone carrying a box for me to stand on – usually much appreciated by the audience.

There are some good reasons to stay behind the podium and some good reasons for moving away from it

Good things

- The microphones are usually built into the podium – generally a pair of them tilted towards you. Leave them alone – do not tap them or speak directly into them. I promise they will be working

- The podium is somewhere to put your speaker notes

- Very often the podium has a glass plate in it with a TV monitor underneath. This allows you to see the slide that is on the screen without having to turn around

Not such good things

- People tend to cling to the podium. This brings rigidity into their style and inhibits good voice projection

- It is more difficult for the audience to see your gestures. This means that you have to put extra effort into the animation and variety in your voice

- Some basic impact techniques, like moving towards the audience for emphasis, are not available to you

So what do I recommend?

I always use a tie clip radio microphone. This is a small microphone that clips to your collar and runs to a box on your waistband. This gives you the option to either stay at the podium or move away as you wish. There are two very important points to remember about these microphones.

Always ask the technician to clip the microphone to the same side of your collar as the screen. In other words if the podium is to the left of the screen then clip it to the right side of your shirt. This is because, even with excellent technique, you will have a tendency to twist towards the screen as you speak and you want to make sure that you are speaking towards the microphone when you do so. This also obviously means that female presenters need to give some thought to what clothes to wear if they are going to use a clip microphone in order to ensure that there is something to fasten it to.

The other and less serious point is that the microphone has a working range of about 25 metres. This is quite far enough to reach from the venue to the bathrooms. So if you have been wired up in advance of your talk please make sure the microphone is switched off before visiting the facilities. I have heard some interesting noises transmitted over the loudspeakers. A CNN reporter visiting the ladies' toilet made headline news in the USA in September 2006 when she broadcast her thoughts about her brother-in-law over the top of a speech by President Bush.

In an ideal world, the stage will have two projection screens positioned left and right both showing your slides. This will allow you to move forward centrally on the stage and deliver your message without blocking anyone's view of the screen. If this is how the stage is set then there will be a spotlight fixed to light you at that location. There will be TV monitors at floor level so you can see your slide without turning around and sometimes there will be another monitor showing a view of you as you appear to the audience.

The screen was so huge and so close, I couldn't see my own slides

The use of monitors in the podium or on the stage will deal with this for you. However, there is also the important issue of how and when your slides will be changed. There are essentially three ways that this can be achieved

- You change the slides

- The technician changes the slides on request

- The technician changes the slides according to the script

You change the slides
This will be by a button operating either a radio link or a wired control and there is usually a forward and back setting. I expected this to be some very high-tech arrangement and I was amused to discover that

very often this is connected to a buzzer or light which signals to the technician to change the slide for you on the computer. This gives you maximum control but of course you may be juggling with a pointer and your notes as well as the slide changer and this can be tricky.

The technician changes the slides on request
This is the "next slide please" approach. It is very clumsy and most audiences find it repetitive and annoying. I do not recommend it especially if your slides contain build ups, each of which would need to be triggered on request.

The technician changes the slides according to the script
If your presentation is complex, perhaps involving embedded video clips, sound effects or where there are two speakers working together on stage at the same time, then you will need to work to a script. The technician will be listening to key words that you deliver and will trigger the slides and effects as you speak. This looks and sounds superbly professional when done well, but clearly depends on a very disciplined approach.

Many speakers would combine this approach with the use of autocue. This is a system that projects the words that you are going to deliver onto a glass plate in front of you. You read these words and can still look directly at the audience. This requires a lot of practice to use well. I recommend that if you are using this system, you have two plates – one slightly to your left and one to your right so that you can change the direction of your gaze whilst still reading the words. To prevent a completely robotic style, occasionally deliver a few words to the centre as well. You will be asked to submit your script well in advance of the event, as someone has to type it into the autocue system. In chapter six you will learn about some of the challenges associated with using a full script. In the context of using an autocue, pay particular attention to using an idiomatic style of writing.

You will want to be as confident as possible when presenting in a large venue. Read the chapter on confidence and use the ideas there, particularly the idea of allocating a specific place on the stage which you feel you own. I always like to walk the stage before the audience arrives and get a sense of its size, how long it takes to walk from one side to the other and whether there are any trip points like steps or cables.

6
Tools of the trade

Anecdotes, metaphors and stories

People love to hear ideas expressed as anecdotes and throughout history, effective communicators have used metaphors as a way of making their message memorable and adding to the impact of what they say.

Unless you already know me, it is very likely that one of the reasons you chose this book was because of its title. The idea of wrestling with a crocodile as a metaphor for the challenge of presenting is much more interesting than making a simple statement that people are often afraid to present.

The Bible uses parables, Aesop wrote his fables. These are books that have stood the test of hundreds if not thousands of years and still have direct relevance today.

Anecdotes can include:

•   Examples from respected sources where the message of the talk has been applied successfully

•   Stories about people who have benefited from whatever it is you are talking about

•   Examples of best practice that you have seen on your travels

If you speak regularly on a specific topic, begin to build a library of anecdotes that you can use in any situation. A speaker representing a shelter for homeless people came to speak to a local charitable trust where I am a member. Their talk on a potentially rather depressing topic was hugely enlivened by stories about the various colourful characters who passed through the shelter at different times of the year.

In general, if you want people to take your advice as a result of your presentation, then it is often better to give the advice as if it were coming from someone else. This removes your ego from the issue. The exception to this is when you are in the position of an expert in your subject and your audience is expecting you to tell them what to do.

For instance I could say:

> *"One of the most effective communication skills techniques I use on a regular basis is to combine good physical skills with a wide range of different rhythms of speech."*

You will inevitably judge this comment based on how you perceive me.

On the other hand, I could say

> *"During my workshops, one of the most effective communication skills techniques I have seen was in Germany, where one of the delegates had a wonderful way of combining physical presentation skills with a wide range of rhythms of speech."*

I am now an impartial observer of someone that you have never met. You are much more likely to accept that this is good advice since I have no vested interest in this delegate. I also gain a valuable additional status by mentioning Germany, which gives me an air of international scope and experience.

A good story needs to be about someone. It takes what would be an abstract third-person series of facts and turns them into something that happened to a real person. This can be someone we all know or someone whose personality and behaviour we either relate to or perhaps even quite strongly reject. We learn as much from the downfall of a villain as we do from the success of a hero.

A good story focuses on how the subject felt as well as on what he did. People respond powerfully to emotionally based stories and to some degree will experience the emotions described. A story that engages at an emotional level will also be much more memorable than one that is simply factual.

The story needs to flow with a clear opening, substance and conclusion. However some of the best storytellers use what is called an "open loop" method. One of the best exponents of this is Billy Connelly who uses the technique to create the illusion of an improvised stream of consciousness when he is on stage. Using this technique, the storyteller sets the scene and takes us into the tale, thereby opening the loop. Instead of concluding the story, the speaker then moves across to start another possibly unrelated story, leaving us wondering about the first one. With skilful delivery, we soon forget the first story and become engrossed in the second, which equally suddenly stops and we are returned with a jolt to the first tale, which concludes, followed then by the conclusion of the second one.

This process of nesting stories inside one another creates a very memorable structure and can be extended to multiple layers.

A good story makes you feel that you were there by evoking all the senses. Remember how I recommended that you "Begin with the end in mind", thinking about what you would be able to see, hear, touch, taste and smell at the conclusion of your successful presentation. A good storyteller creates all these for the listener.

A good story is a drama. I recently had the experience of watching a professional Irish storyteller recount the tale of Noah's ark to a group of young children. We were in the saloon of the wonderful tall ship "Tenacious" which is owned by the Jubilee Sailing Trust to help disabled people experience the thrill of sailing. We were in Dublin for a tall ship regatta and the ship had been turned over to these young people. We all know the story of Noah's ark; I am an adult and was expecting to be bored. I stayed for every moment, watching as the gestures, timing and vocal richness of this actor brought the topic and all the characters to life. It wasn't the story that held me; it was the complete commitment of the storyteller to the words that kept me there.

Crocodile Summary

- Anecdotes and stories can transform an otherwise boring topic

- Build your library of personal anecdotes

- Usually use third person examples rather than positioning yourself as the source of all good ideas

- Engage your audience at an emotional level

What is that button for?

I know that this chapter is likely to cause me to produce a second edition of this book faster than anything else. Technology moves on apace. Let's deal with some principles first before looking at specific items.

Every tool or gadget should be used because it in some way adds to the impact or quality of your presentation. This is the only reason to use it. Gadgets are more likely to detract from your presentation rather than add to it so use them sparingly.

Gadgets fall into four categories

•   Pointing devices

•   Data projectors

•   Slide changers

•   Writing tools

Pointing devices

My personal feeling about these devices is to avoid using them if possible. Verbal navigation around the image is often just as effective

> *"Please take a look at the blue line on the chart"*
>
> *"Please concentrate on the middle column on the table"*

That said they can be very effective if used sparingly and remember that a significant minority of people, especially men, are colour blind.

Most people seem to use pointers too much and also they seem to be obsessed with keeping pointing whilst they are talking about what they are pointing at.

The trick is to separate the elements ....

I call the technique for effective use of a laser pointer

- Point

- Pivot

- Deliver

Most people try to keep the laser spot or other pointer on the screen whilst explaining what it is they are pointing at. This is impossible. If you do this you will either:

- Talk to the screen because you are looking where the pointer is directed

- Talk to the audience and so have no idea where the pointer is aiming

The secret is to realise that effective use of a pointer is more like someone going up to the screen, tapping briefly on a point and then moving away, rather than a permanent direction towards the point.

Try this

> *Find an image with a graph or table on it*
>
> *Turn to the slide in silence and point to the element you want the audience to look at. Use a circular movement to conceal any inaccuracy in your aim at the screen.*
>
> *Now pivot away from the slide to face your audience. Ignore your own slide completely.*
>
> *Now deliver the message. The audience will remember where you have pointed. There is no need to keep the pointer on the slide.*

If you are not using the pointer, it is preferable for you to put it down.

There are three main types of pointing device

- Laser pointers

- Telescopic pointers

- Software pointers

Laser pointers project a bright red spot of light onto a screen. The pointer can be a pen-like device or it can be built into the remote control of a data projector.

Laser pointers magnify any nervous tremor in your hand so use them sparingly and very briefly, just long enough to make the point.

Telescopic pointers are an underrated tool. These look like a pen but they extend like an old fashioned car aerial. They can be quite effective when you are presenting to small groups. Always be aware though that as you approach the screen to point to something, you run the risk of turning away from your audience and you inevitably will be moving away from them. All of this can reduce your impact. Use the pointer sparingly and move back towards the audience as soon as you can.

PowerPoint has embedded pointing and writing tools. When you are in slide show mode, a right click of the mouse will pull up a menu and allow you to select an arrow that you can move over your slide to indicate a point. You can also pull up a pen tool allowing you to write on the slide or highlight points. It goes without saying that keeping good eye contact with the audience, using powerful gestures and playing with various mouse buttons is quite a trick and unless you are really practised or have an unusually complex point to make, it is probably best avoided.

Projection Equipment

Data projectors are a routine tool for presenters and projector technology changes almost by the week. The underlying purpose is always the same – to allow you to project PowerPoint slides onto a screen. A modern data projector has one huge advantage over older projection systems and that is that it is so bright that you can keep normal room lighting levels when you are using it. The differences in technology tend to be in the way that the information is moved from your computer to the projector. Direct cable connections between PC and projector are giving way to wireless connections and to the ability to plug a USB memory stick into the projector and so dispense with the PC altogether. All of these developments mean that you have greater choice of where you position yourself relative to the audience and the equipment. With a conventional cable connection you are literally tied to the projector by the 1 or 2 metres of VGA cable running between the computer and the projector.

A word about who the various images are intended to benefit. Always remember that the image on the main screen is entirely for the audience. The image on your PC screen is for you. The impression that you want to try and create is that you have a complete and comprehensive knowledge of your materials and so do not need to look at the main screen as a reminder. This effect is best achieved by placing the PC so that you can see your PC screen, maintain eye contact with the audience and also not block the view of the projected image by the audience members nearest to you.

You can now engage your audience and have a reminder of the content of the slides without turning to look. This gives a very professional impression.

Slide changers

A quick tour of the duty free shops or the computer shops on the High Street will show you how many different types of mouse you can buy. This is important because you will either change slides by operating the PC directly from the keyboard or you will use some sort of adapted mouse. It is better to give yourself as much flexibility as possible and that probably means that you should invest in some sort of radio mouse. This consists of a small receiver that plugs into the USB socket of the computer and allows you to change slides with a compact unit that you hold in your hand. This can be a full mouse with the ability to select programs or a simpler gadget that just enables you to move forwards and backwards through your presentation. It may well incorporate a laser pointer.

Whatever device you use, only keep it in your hand when you need to. Anything that you hold carries the risk of becoming a toy that you twist and turn and which reveals any nervousness. It will also tend to suppress your gestures. If you are not using it, put it down.

Every data projector comes equipped with a remote controller. This can also be used to change slides but more importantly it has two functions, blank and freeze.

When you press the blank button the projector screen turns black but you can still see the slide on your PC screen. This allows you to check the next slide or skip over slides without the audience seeing what is happening. Press it again to reveal the image. The freeze button is even cleverer. It locks the current image onto the screen whilst allowing you to change slides on your PC. When you press the button again, the image jumps to the one on your PC screen.

If the remote control is missing, a good second best is to press the B key on your keyboard whilst in PowerPoint slide show mode – the screen will go blank but so will your PC screen. This is very useful when you are asked a question to enable you to quickly remove the distraction of an image whilst you deal with the issue.

Use the remote controller to blank and freeze images. The B key is a good second option

Overhead Projector

A much older but still quite widely used tool is the overhead projector. I like these machines although they are likely to disappear over the next few years.

Their advantages are:

*   The image is bright and can be seen in normal room lighting

*   They can be used dynamically to create a visual in front of the audience by writing on a blank acetate sheet

*   Because of the way the images are projected, when pointing to an acetate on the plate of an overhead projector, you will be facing your audience, which is clearly an advantage

Do not try to put too much information on each transparency; no more than about 20 words or three or four clearly distinguished curves on each one.

Using the silhouette of a pen you can point to the particular items on the visual, but do not hold the pen. Lay it flat it on the projector, as any trembling of your hand will be magnified on the screen. Remember to keep out of the line of sight between the screen and the person in the audience who is nearest to you.

When you have finished with a transparency, turn the machine off so that the audience looks at you. Put the next transparency on the projector and switch on again when the next visual is needed and not before.

Store the transparencies in a plastic pocket that can be put away in a ring-file. These pockets are convenient to transport and can be numbered or used for notes. Do not punch holes in the transparency itself as these will show up on the screen when you project it.

There are widely varying opinions about slow reveal techniques with an overhead projector. This is the technique where a list of information is on the transparency and a piece of paper is used to gradually reveal it. I personally hate this technique because of the potential pitfalls. I have lost count of the number of times someone has placed the transparency on the machine, thereby showing the entire contents to the audience and then covered it up. The piece of paper being used usually drops off the glass plate about four rows from the bottom of the list, assuming the fan in the projector hasn't blown it away. Add to this the fact that in order to manipulate the sheet of paper, the speaker will probably be blocking everyone's view of the screen and you might be able to see where my opinions come from.

Tablet PCs

A new development, which is starting to be more common, is the tablet PC. This is similar to a normal laptop in appearance. The difference is that the screen detaches from the keyboard base and converts to a touch sensitive panel that communicates with the base using a radio link. The best designed of these have the connection to a projector built into the base. This means that a presenter can stand anywhere in the room and use the tablet to control the presentation. The touch sensitive aspect allows the presenter to sketch on the tablet and the drawn image appears on the projected screen. As wireless links between computer and projector become more common, this is probably the technological way of the future.

Flip Chart

The final display tool is the extremely low-tech but very useful flip chart. This is the most valuable visual aid for anyone who is genuinely facilitating a discussion. It is quick, cheap and easy to use and outputs from it can be permanently displayed around the walls of the room.

There is something pre-packaged about even the best designed PowerPoint presentation and a very effective technique is to mix in a few flip chart sheets to create a sense of "breaking news" and spontaneity. There are some very good workshops on how to make the best use of flip charts but as someone who is artistically challenged to say the least, the one trick I use regularly is to prepare flip sheets in advance by drawing diagrams and figures very lightly in pencil. At the appropriate moment I trace over the lines with a flip pen, thus guaranteeing that the diagram is centred and fits on the page.

The most important audio-visual tool

More critical than any of these gadgets, tools and techniques is the realisation that the most important piece of audio-visual equipment in the room is you.

Every time you show a PowerPoint slide or put up an acetate, you are taking the audience's attention away from the source of the real power in the room which is you.

It is absolutely not necessary to support every comment or point with some sort of image. Your excellent physical and vocal technique can have more impact and be memorable than any slide.

If you are given the choice, there is an optimal way to position the projection equipment relative to you and the audience. That is with the screen placed across the corner of the room with you placed centrally in front of the people.

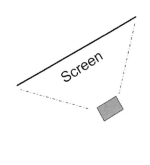

This arrangement means that when the audience faces forwards they are looking at you. You can then control when they look off to one side to view the slides. An additional advantage of this layout is that all the audience members will be able to see the screen with no risk of you blocking them.

Unfortunately this set-up is not always possible as the room may be prepared before you arrive, or more commonly the screen is fixed to a flat wall and cannot be moved.

Crocodile Summary

*   All equipment should support your objective, not hinder it

*   There is no requirement to have a PowerPoint slide for every idea

*   Set up the room to make it easy for your audience to see both you and your images.

What was it I was going to say?

There are many different ways of helping yourself remember what to say and when to say it. These range from a full script right through to relying on your memory (which is what actors have to do!).

One significant confidence builder is to realise that the only person who knows what you were planning to say is you. I think it is probably true that I have never stood in front of an audience and delivered exactly the words that I have been practicing. What I do always deliver though is the overall message that I have planned and that is what matters. So if you miss a point out along the way, put it in somewhere else or forget about it as long as it is not essential. Never tell the audience that you have missed something out.

Here are my thoughts on the various tools and techniques available to you.

Full script

Not a bad place to start if you do not deliver presentations very often. The problem is that most people use a different style of language when they write to when they speak and the written word can sound rather wooden when it is spoken out loud. If you do want to work off a full script then write it idiomatically using words like "can't" and "won't" which you would never use in a piece of normal writing. It is also difficult to keep your place in a script and still work with the audience and your visuals. Every time you look at the audience you risk losing your way amongst the paper.

I prefer to use a script as a starting point back in the office. It allows me to time a presentation fairly accurately. I use one of the other techniques to help me keep track of my talk when I am actually in front of my audience.

PowerPoint Notes pages

If you are using PowerPoint, there is a useful function that allows you to write your words under the visual when you are designing the talk. You then print these off and you always know which words go with which image. This is a lot better than the mass of words which constitute a script but there is still a danger of writing too much down for you to be able to work with it in front of the audience.

Cue cards

These take advantage of the fact that all you really need is a topic prompt to get you going rather than having every word written down. Cue cards are large postcards – one per key idea or per visual and the significant words are marked on them in as large a print as possible. You can use PowerPoint notes pages in a similar way. This is my preferred approach. It combines simplicity and ease of use with a good solid reminder to help keep you on track and maintain your confidence. It is very easy to drop cue cards so either number them or punch the corners and put in a treasury tag to keep them in order.

Look or Speak?

A fundamental technique of professional speakers is to realise that the rule of only speaking when you are looking at someone applies equally well when you are working with a script or cue cards.

If you look at the notes as you speak, you will draw the attention of the audience to the fact that you are reading and this creates the impression that you are unsure of your content. It tends to break your authority and risks damaging the relationship you are building with the people out in the audience.

Instead, follow this simple flow

Look at the audience and introduce the next slide/visual

> *"I would like to move on now to consider the performance of this new motorbike"*

Now stop talking, look at your notes and remind yourself what the next point is supposed to be – take your time, it isn't taking as long as you think.

Now look up, engage with someone in the audience and deliver your next sentence.

Because you are always looking at someone when you speak, the cue cards seem to disappear into the background and you will come across as a professional and well-informed speaker.

In practice, once you are into your presentation flow, you will often find that you do not need to refer to your cards at all.

Crocodile Summary

•   Rehearse thoroughly

•   Practice answering likely questions

•   Prepare cue cards if they will help your confidence – some of the best speakers in the world use them

•   Use your presenting skills to minimise the impact of cue cards

7
Be prepared

Practice until it looks like you haven't had to practice

This section contains some good advice about rehearsal and some tips to help you when you are actually out there in front of the audience.

Morecambe and Wise and the Two Ronnies are two examples of the most enduring and professional British comedy acts of the late 20th century. They (especially Morecambe and Wise) had an act that appeared to be littered with errors and improvisations. Nothing could be further from the truth. Every hesitation, every stumble was carefully scripted and rehearsed until it looked spontaneous. A more modern example is The Office, where the fly on the wall, documentary style was a carefully designed fakery.

The message here is that there is no substitute for practice. Your minimum target should be to be so familiar with your words and visuals that you have sufficient spare mental capacity to be thinking about your physical and vocal presenting technique.

True, this advice is of little help for off the cuff presenting but this is relatively rarely needed. The majority of talks are given after plenty of notice and time to prepare.

Practise on your friends and family. Make sure they know that you want honest feedback and tips for improvement. The last thing you need is someone who is trying to be nice and doesn't tell you where you need to change things.

Tape your presentation – possibly on video and certainly on audio tape and listen to it carefully. If you don't have a video camera then present to a mirror. Forget your accent, forget how you look in terms of your height, weight, hair colour and style. If some fashion tips come out of the exercise then that is a useful bonus but it isn't the purpose. You should be considering the points listed on the next few pages. This is also a useful summary of the core skills described in this book:

Stance

Desirable behaviours
*   Feet hip width apart, toes slightly turned out

*   Well grounded, keeping still

*   Weight evenly distributed

Common faults
*   Feet touching

*   Feet too far apart

*   Toes parallel

*   Toes turned in

*   Toes turned out excessively

*   Pacing

*   Wobbling

*   Standing on one leg

*   Weight on one hip

Gestures

Desirable behaviours
*   Hands relaxed and loose at the sides when not in use

*   Hands relaxed and held gently at just above waist height when not in use

*   Gestures always above the waist

*   Gestures from the shoulder not the elbow

*   Appropriate width of gesture for audience size

Common faults

- Hands held rigidly by the sides

- Hands gripped tightly together

- Hands in pockets

- Hands behind back

- Small gestures below the waist

- Gestures from the elbow

Eye contact

Desirable behaviours

- Holding contact for "one thought"

- Involving everyone

- Random direction

Common faults

- No eye contact

- Fleeting eye contact

- Staring

- Regular predictable pattern

Voice

Desirable behaviours

- Varying pitch, pace and volume for effect

- Using pauses for emphasis

- Projecting to the rear of the audience

Common faults

*   Too fast

*   Speaking to the front row

*   Lack of variation

*   Too quiet

Question Technique

Desirable behaviours

*   Paraphrase to confirm understanding

*   Replying to everyone

*   Moving forward for tough questions

Common faults

*   Only speaking to the questioner

*   Responding too quickly

*   Assuming you understand the question

Most people practice their presentation to some extent. It is just as important that you practice how you will answer likely questions. You know the material and the topic much more thoroughly than the audience and so there is no doubt that you will know what they are likely to ask. Think about this in advance and decide what you will say. You might want to include something in the main part of the talk to head off a particularly tricky challenge.

Let Me at 'Em!

This book is about the methods I use to give people professional, powerful and assured presenting techniques. As the delegates I work with develop a better and better technique, I see them grow in confidence over a few hours and I receive regular feedback saying that this has carried on back in the real world. Many people who I work with have had a lifetime's sense of being afraid of speaking in front of audiences. The experience of feeling that fear replaced by a quiet confidence and then real enjoyment is a very powerful one for them.

This is probably the most challenging part of what I do to express in print but the method is built around a few simple ideas, many of which you will recognise as being drawn from the core techniques I have described earlier in the book.

- Build on belief

- You are not your content

- Going there first

- Breathing

- Physiology

- Location

- Anchors

- Pace

- Pause

Build on belief

There is an intangible sense of authenticity that surrounds an excellent presenter who is performing well. It is driven by a genuine passion and belief in what they are saying. If you were to use the techniques described in this book to deliver a presentation on a subject you really didn't believe in, then it would show. Something about your timing and about the inflection in your voice would give it away.

So what does that mean in practice? It means that you must think carefully about your objective and about your message. Is it really going to benefit your audience? Is it important to you and them to receive your message? Are you comfortable with the content that you are delivering?

If the answer to any of these is no then you should reassess whether to make the presentation or review the content.

You are not your content

In nearly every situation, your audience will want you to do well. It is an enjoyable experience to watch someone present with confidence and clarity. This is entirely separate from whether they agree with you. You may deliver the most assured presentation and then have a very heated discussion. This is good news. It means that you communicated with such power that you reached someone at an emotional level and they responded. Their powerful response will nearly always be aimed at what you are saying NOT AT YOU.

If you feel that the questions or discussion is becoming too personal for your comfort then turn the topic into a third party issue. For instance, returning to the charity scenario, someone might say to me:

> *"Stuart, you are defending the indefensible. You are adopting an approach to charitable work that will break the bank"*

The use of my name and the direct criticism of my action is getting a little personal so I look for a point of agreement; in this case that we both want to do good charitable work. I then use a physical technique that I call triangulation. To do this I look at the person concerned, make a statement of agreement and then define where we disagree. At the same time I move my hands to a point off to one side of both of us, looking to where my hands are pointing. Something like:

	"I think we are agreed on one thing, that we both want to achieve as much as possible for our respective charitable causes.
Point off to one side	*What we need to do is to find a way to agree on the best way to manage expenditure"*

The other person will usually look where your hands are pointing and the sense of personal pressure on you will disappear.

Going there first

Let's expand on the idea that people like to see you do well as a speaker. To go there first means you have to know what the audience would like from you. You already do know this. They want someone to speak to them who is confident, relaxed and in control. The fun bit is that they will decide this from what they see you doing and what you say.

They cannot see inside you. So all you have to do is **look** sufficiently confident, relaxed and in control until they decide that you are all of these and they will then respond to you in a very positive way. You can then ride on this until you genuinely do feel positive. However, you have to go there first.

This powerful concept is based on the work of Dr Susan Jeffers who expressed the idea in her wonderful book "Feel the Fear – and do it anyway".

So, what do you do? You combine elements of everything I have described so far. The audience decides what it believes about you in the time it takes you to walk from your chair to the place where you will speak. Take advantage of this.

- Breathe gently outwards – more about this in a moment

- Walk steadily to the centre of the stage or platform

- Pause for a mental count of two seconds

- Smile, and as you say good morning and give your name, cast your eyes across the audience

The controlled and methodical feel that this sequence will generate will create all the positive impressions that you will need to put the audience on your side.

Breathing

The most important contribution you can make to your confidence is by managing your breathing. Most presenters breathe in as they

For the budding storytellers amongst you, this section closes a loop about confident presenting that I opened back in the introduction

approach the stage or podium and they then do something that I call "breathing from a full chest". This means that they keep their lungs full and their chest expanded and then they breathe in a very shallow way without emptying their lungs properly between breaths. This has a series of unfortunate effects:

- The levels of carbon dioxide in the blood start to rise, this creates a tense, anxious feeling

- There is little airflow through the larynx so the voice weakens and becomes quiet

- The muscles in the shoulders and back tighten

Stand up now and try it.

> *Breathe in, hold that full chest and start to speak – recite a nursery rhyme. After a few seconds you will feel the tension build. When you are really aware of this, breathe out slowly and deeply. You may be surprised at how a sense of relaxation spreads through not just your chest but also your whole body.*

It is clear from this little demonstration that the correct technique is to breathe out as you walk to the centre of the stage, rather than breathe in. It is that slow exhalation as you walk out to the place where you are going to give your talk that will relax you, empower your voice and allow you to deliver at your peak.

Physiology

Your body and your brain are inextricably linked. How you feel affects how you use your body – we all know that. The reverse is also true. How you use your body affects how you feel about a situation.

Try this exercise.

> *Stand up, spread your arms wide, smile and look up towards the ceiling about three metres away. Now try to feel miserable. Not easy is it? That is because the physiology of a miserable person is hunched, closed and downward looking. Your brain is taking its orders from your body and your body is behaving in a positive, optimistic way.*

Now, ask yourself this question:

> *Thinking back to the most effective and professional presentation you have ever seen, how was the presenter standing? How did she hold her body and where was she looking?*
>
> *Stand up again and now model that behaviour. You may need to adapt it a bit to feel comfortable but make sure you keep the elements that were the most powerful for you. Over time, you can now develop the habit of adopting that physiology just before you start a presentation. It's just like checking your tie, glancing in the mirror to make sure your hair is OK or that your lipstick isn't smeared – make sure you have adopted your confident presenter look.*

Modelling behaviour is a technique that all children use. It is how they learn to do all of the everyday things we take for granted like holding a knife and fork or riding a bicycle. As adults we tend to lose our ability to do this because we develop a fear of failure and we also do not use good observational skills. To get better at anything you have to do it and when you are learning, you will get it wrong a lot of the time. You will learn every time and you will get better every time.

If you want to be an excellent presenter, you can do no better than to go and watch as many professional presenters as you can. When you do this, go further than just getting a general impression of their quality. Ask yourself what it is they are actually doing that is working for them and decide how you can use the same techniques yourself.

Location

A technique that many excellent presenters use is to mentally mark out the presenting area and allocate different tasks to each area. For instance, there may be a place quite near your PC where you feel confident presenting data. On the other hand, you may decide that there is a place more or less in the centre of the stage where you feel you can reach the audience and can respond well to questions. It can be very powerful to work out where these places are before the audience arrives and always to return to that spot to deliver a particular part of your presentation. It makes the presenting space much more comfortable and can give you a sense of control and ownership of it.

Anchors

Confident presenters constantly remind themselves of the great times they have had working with audiences. Unsurprisingly, these thoughts make them feel even better and their presenting becomes more and more effective.

Presenters who have not yet built their confidence tend to spend their time recalling when they didn't feel good about presenting. Since it is a well known fact that your brain will reinforce what you spend time thinking about, this is clearly not a good idea.

That's fine you might say, but I haven't yet delivered a great presentation and so I haven't got any good stuff to think about. Fortunately this doesn't matter. What you need to do is build yourself an anchor.

Anchors are everywhere. They are something that reminds you of the way that you felt at some time in the past. By thinking of it, you can feel that way again.

Every time I smell a frying breakfast, I instantly feel everything good about family camping holidays as a child. The sense of fun, anticipation and pleasure comes flooding back in an instant as a result of that one simple stimulus. That is an anchor that has happened to me by chance. You can benefit by building anchors deliberately.

Try this. You might want to read it all the way through first so you understand the whole exercise.

Stand in your most confident presenter stance. Now, think back to a time when you were at your most confident. I don't mean as a presenter, I mean in any situation in your life. Now take your time and think through all your senses and build up the reality of that memory.

- *What could you see?*

- *What noises were there – not just voices but passing traffic or the sound of machinery?*

- *What could you feel – what was your mood, what was the*

> *occasion. Were you wearing a favourite outfit or favourite shoes?*
>
> •   *What could you smell? Were you wearing a particular perfume or after-shave?*
>
> •   *What could you taste? What had you had for breakfast or lunch? Had you been eating a mint?*
>
> *As your sense of the situation reaches its peak take the index finger of one hand and press quite firmly on the back of your other hand. Now imagine if you could take that confident and wonderful feeling and just like the volume slider on an amplifier increase the feeling tenfold. So do it – keep the pressure on your hand and slide your index finger all the way to the tip of one of the fingers, feeling your confidence build as you do so.*

This technique is called building an anchor. Every time something good happens to you and you feel confident and powerful, repeat that sliding action. Very quickly, your brain will associate that movement with feeling confident and positive.

Remember though that an anchor is just like your pet crocodile. It needs regular feeding. Make sure you keep reinforcing it.

That's how to build an anchor. Now how to use it.

Just before you start your presentation, repeat the sliding movement. You brain will recognise this and will instantly release the sense of confidence and power that you have built into it. This will place you in the right frame of mind to present at your absolute best.

Many people find that music is a very powerful trigger to other senses and to memories. If this is the case for you then play a piece of music that has a positive meaning for you just before you deliver your presentation. If you have a portfolio of complimentary letters and emails that people have sent you then read it just before you step onto the stage. It doesn't matter what the topic is as long as the comments are positive.

Pace and Pause

These are two old friends from earlier in the book. You know how to use them and it is important to understand as well how they can support your confidence as a presenter.

Confident presenters take their time. They allow their ideas to sink into the mind of the audience. They allow the audience time to think. A measured pace with plenty of pauses also gives you time to think and to breathe. As you present, self-check to make sure you are allowing two second pauses between ideas.

Remember, use speed as an energiser in the less important links between sections of your presentation. Use pace and pause where you want the idea to sink in and where you want to make sure the audience knows you are in control.

Personal Preparation

Dress

My delegates can sometimes become very concerned about personal appearance. To maximise your confidence you need to dress in a way that makes you feel comfortable, in control and therefore confident.

As a general rule of thumb:

Dress one step more formally than your audience. If they are in jeans, then wear smart casual trousers. If they are in open neck shirts then wear a tie but probably not a business suit. Please leave the novelty tie for Christmas day.

This is a very broad generalisation and only applies if you want to come across in an authoritative way. If your objective relates more to building a close rapport with your audience then you may choose to dress in the same way as them.

Only fasten your jacket if it is a good fit. Many people, both men and women buy tailored jackets that they wear unbuttoned and they look very smart. Unfortunately when fastened they are so tight that they restrict breathing and make the owner look very tense. Take a look in a mirror or ask a friend for an honest opinion and don't feel you have to literally be all buttoned up.

Avoid distracting jewellery particularly bangles which are very audible every time you move. It can be very disconcerting to realise that you sound like a percussion orchestra.

Use the Bathroom

One of the effects of adrenaline is to speed up the rate of movement of the contents of your digestive system. This has inevitable effects. Every speaker makes more frequent visits to the bathroom just before a talk than they would normally. Don't fight it. Plan for it and make sure you are comfortable when you stand up to deliver your presentation.

Watch what you drink

This applies to both alcoholic and non-alcoholic drinks. It is not my place to tell you whether or not to have an alcoholic drink before presenting. What I can tell you is that there are two guaranteed effects. The positive one is that you will be physically more relaxed. The negative one is that this relaxation comes at the expense of loss of concentration and focus and a reduced ability to read the audience's reactions accurately. I personally never drink alcohol before delivering any sort of a talk but I reach with a deep sigh of relief and satisfaction for a glass of wine afterwards.

Non-alcoholic drinks also present their challenges

Carbonated drinks
These place you at risk of the dreaded burp at the most inappropriate times in your talk. Remember as well that many contain caffeine, which is a powerful diuretic, and so the bathroom problems described above become an issue again.

Milk
Avoid any drink containing milk. Milk has a strange effect on the throat. It encourages the mouth to produce thickened saliva, which affects the sound of the voice and results in reduced projection. The same applies to very cold iced drinks of any sort.

The best thing to drink before a presentation is cool still water with a twist of lemon or lime.

Crocodile summary

*   Every presenter feels apprehensive. You would not do well if you felt totally calm.

*   Above all – make sure you breathe and take your time.

*   Prepare physically as well as mentally

Pulling it all together

You may well have been wondering why this book seems to pay so little attention to the quality of the content of your presentations. There are two reasons, one of which you will probably accept and the other of which may surprise you.

The first reason is that I am assuming that you know your subject. The techniques that I teach are designed to maximise the impact of reasonable messages delivered by well-informed presenters.

The second reason is that the content is the least important part of your presentation. But, I hear you cry, "I am here to deliver a message and that message is my content".

But is it?

The reason for you being here, preparing to present, is so that you can achieve the objective of your talk. As we have already discussed, that may be to change opinions, encourage people to do things or make people think and even if it is just to inform them, you need to do so in a way that motivates them to listen.

Any of you who have been to scientific conferences or even had to listen to lectures in school, college or university will have encountered an awful sensation. It's the one where you know that the lecture content is important to you and is probably wonderfully intelligent stuff but because the presenter has such terrible technique you cannot take in the message.

Professor Albert Mehrabian is frequently quoted when this topic is discussed. He originated the famous 7/38/55 rule, which is represented in this diagram.

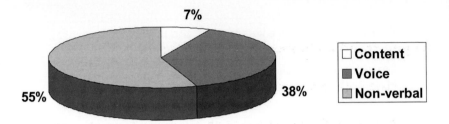

- •   7% of the impact of a presentation comes from the content

- •   38% from the voice

- •   55% from the non-verbal behaviour of the presenter

In fairness to the Professor, he was actually examining what contributed to people's like or dislike of messages rather than their impact. There is no doubt though that the majority of the impact of a presentation comes from something other than the content itself.

For those of you who have delivered presentations before, take a moment and do a quick reality check. You decided on the content, you designed the slides and you practiced. We have established that something over 80% of the impact of a talk comes from factors other than the content. On that basis you will have spent lots of time deciding where to put in a gesture, where to drop the volume of your voice, where to take a pace forward…. didn't you?

It is essential that you deliver your message with what is described as congruence. This simply means that every aspect of your communica-tion must deliver the same message with the same degree of conviction. The most important time in your presentation is the first few seconds. This is where the people in the audience make up their mind about you and then spend the rest of the time trying to prove to themselves that they were right.

This is where you must apply all the techniques we have discussed to their maximum effect.

The next page or so is my quick reference guide for the whole book. There is a lot of information in *Wrestling with Crocodiles* and a lot of tips and techniques. The points listed below are the ones that have made the biggest difference for me and continue to do so.

You need to be at your best in the first few seconds of your presentation

As you stand up in front of the audience:

•   Have nothing distracting up on the screen

•   Mentally begin your presentation before you stand up – no fidgeting

•   Breathe out as you walk from your chair

•   Pause before speaking and take in all of the audience

•   Smile

•   As you speak your first few words, make an inclusive gesture

Then move into the structure of your talk – focusing on the attention grabber

As you deliver your presentation:

•   Keep your objective in mind

•   Keep your attention on your audience – look for the positive responses

•   Keep breathing

•   Keep a controlled pace

As you end your presentation:

•   Shift your energy to revitalise the audience

•   Deliver a clear, unambiguous call for action

As you manage questions and discussion:

•   Keep focused on your objective

•   Feel confident to end the Q&A or discussion any time you feel like it

•   Always have the last word and recap your objective

•   Stay in "presenter mode" until you are sitting down again

Celebrate your success. Reflect on what went well and make sure you do it again.

Reflect on what could have gone better – I have been presenting for more than 25 years and I learn something every time.

The sense of satisfaction and achievement that comes from having delivered a successful presentation is hard to describe. You will be surprised at how energised you are after speaking, and how tired.

Enjoy working with audiences and may the crocodile go with you.

Additional Reading

These are a few additional resources that you might like to look at. Some of them are mentioned in the book, others have acted as an inspiration to me in other ways.

Feel the fear and do it anyway
Susan Jeffers.   Pub: Rider Books, ISBN: 0-7126-7105-6

This is the book that contains the wonderfully simple idea that every time you do something new, you will be apprehensive. Once you have done it successfully, the fear goes away and is replaced by a sense of achievement. To progress in life you have to constantly face new challenges and deal with the apprehension before enjoying the success. This is truer of presenting than of almost any other activity.

A voice of your own (Video tape)
Patsy Rodenburg.   Pub: Vanguard Productions, PO Box 70,
                            Norwich NR1 2ED

Patsy Rodenburg is a leading voice coach to the professional theatre. As well as tapes, she has several published books including "The right to speak" and "The need for words" both published by Methuen.

The seven habits of highly effective people
Stephen R Covey   Pub: Simon and Schuster, ISBN: 0-671-71117-2

This book is a constant source of inspiration and ideas. Probably the best of the modern self-improvement books, it was the source for my quote "Begin with the end in mind" used to advise you on planning your presentation.

Training with NLP
Joseph O'Connor
and John Seymour   Pub: Thorsons, ISBN: 0-72225-2853-1

The principles that I use to design my workshops and to ensure that they meet the needs of the many different people who attend, are grounded in my training as a practitioner of neurolinguistic programming (NLP). I am often asked for further reading on the subject and this book is a useful and non-technical route to understanding how NLP can work in practice. If your interest is in an area other than training and communication then browse though the web site of Anglo American books who have a huge range of different publications centred on the theme of NLP. They can be found at www.anglo-american.co.uk.

The mind map book: Radiant thinking
Tony Buzan   Pub: BBC Active, ISBN: 0-56348-7011

Tony Buzan invented mind mapping, which along with other creative thinking techniques such as brainstorming should be the starting point for the design of your presentations. He is a prolific author and this is one of many excellent books for learning about the topic.

Index